INCREASE YOUR VALUE

(Net Worth)

Oluwafemi Dennis Ojo

Seekers Publishers

ISBN-13: 9798724483766
ISBN-10: 1477123456

Cover design by: xpro graphic Art
Library of Congress Control Number: 2018675309
Printed in the United States of America

CONTENTS

PREFACE

Your value determines your level of acceptability and worth in the society. Knowledge is not static nor the earth stagnant. Both of them are dynamic, as they are dynamic so man needs to be dynamic in increasing his worth or value daily. The way you were last year, last month or last week is no longer enough to make you valuable today, this week, this month or this year. Someone may have studied you and improve on your product or what you've done. He will be the talk of the town and all attention will be on him and not you.

We need to daily seek ways to increase our value. The world is no longer the way God created when the beginning began.. Does it occur to you that so many features have been added on the face of the earth? These features have made the earth more valuable and beautiful than the time God created it. If the earth was said to be very good then as recorded in Gen1: 31, what will you say about it now? Gloriously beautiful.

This book is inspired to boast or stir up your mind so you can begin to work on your value daily. Whatever achievements you've achieved has gone with yesterday. How will you want people to see you today? Tomorrow is yet another day new people with new products, achievements, potentials and capacity will be introducing and you will no longer be relevant. No matter how hard you wash your Mercedes Benz 200 1986 model and you brought it out thinking people will celebrate you as they did in that year when this car was invoke. You will end up discover that your value and that of the car means nothing to the world of today. Stop celebrating yesterday, that is a pass glory.

Start working on how great you want people to see you and value you and be mindful of various value killers as you keep in view the lives of great people who have impacted life in the past that your life must be better than theirs. This act will make your net worth increase significantly.

As you read this book I believed God that your level will change and new inspirations will be stir up in your mind and a new drive to reach new height will be birth in you. Your name will end up as one of those men and women who were relevant in the world in your own time.

Oluwafemi Dennis Ojo N.C.E, BSc, Pgd, M.Th, D.D

CHAPTER ONE

THE ORIGINAL MAN

The original man created by God in Genesis chapter one was a man filled with all manner of potentials and abilities. God doesn't intend a man like robot as we have today. Who must be remote controlled and doesn't have mind of his own. To show this, he finished creating all things before He made man. All other things were created through the word of God but man was made with God going out to work shop to be worked on. The created things; plant, animals and other elements were to assist man to function in his full potentials. The garden of Eden(World) was designed by God for man to carry out his specific assignments.

"And the Lord took the man and put him into the garden of Eden to <u>DRESS</u> it and to <u>KEEP</u> it"

Gen 2: 15 KJV

"Then the Lord placed the man in the garden of Eden to <u>CULTIVATE</u> it and to <u>GUARD</u> it"

Gen2:15 GNV

The word dress, cultivate, keep and guard connote responsibility. Man, was to care for the garden and put into full use for his advantage and to the glory of God. These responsibilities were expressed in God's statement before He made man.

"And God said, let us <u>MAKE</u> man in our image, after our likeness and let them have dominion over the fish of the sea, and over the fowl of the air and over the cattle, and over all the air and over every creeping things that creep upon the earth"

Gen1:26 KJV

God created man in His image and likeness, so man created possesses what God has. Man, has the mind of God, abilities, thoughts and his reasoning power. The created man possesses the managerial skills to administer the whole garden in all wisdom. Adam was able to distinguish and categories all animals, trees, grasses, fishes and birds and gave them names accordingly.

"God created man in his image and likeness, so man created possess what God possesses. Man, has the mind of God, abilities, thoughts and his reasoning power. The created man possesses the managerial skills to administer the whole garden in all wisdom. Adam was able to distinguish and categories all animals, trees, grasses, fishes and birds and gave them names accordingly. "

Gen2:19-20 KJV

The mind power of man was so deep and rich in all knowledge, understanding and wisdom that he was able to invent names for all things created. The names were never in existence but Adam invented them from his deep mind the same way God created all things from the His deepest mind (imagination). Everything including man came from God's imagination. That we can see in the above passage.

"... even <u>God, who gives life to the dead and calls into existence things that don't yet exist</u>"

Rom4:17 ISV

God and man manifested the same abilities at creation. This is because man possess the Spirit of God. This make it easy for man to create names and what God had in mind was what Adam came up with and it became acceptable to God. God acknowledged this as he gave name to everything created by God. God must have been very happy to see man manifest all His abilities. It takes the help of the functional Spirit of God in Adam to know the mind of God concerning the naming of all things. The spirit of God in Adam was alive and active. This spirit in man connects with that of to give us the mind of God at every point of decision making.

"But God has revealed those things to us by his SPIRIT, for the SPIRIT searches, everything, even the deep things of God. Is there anyone who can understand his own thoughts except his own inner spirit? In the same way, no one can know the thoughts of God except God's SPIRIT."

1Cor 2:10–11 ISV

"The SPIRIT of man is the candle of the LORD, searching all the inward parts of the belly"

Pro 20:27 KJV

The living Spirit of God transfers through His breath into Adam, makes him see things like God, reason like God and makes him a supernatural being like God. Through the SPIRIT he was able to see into the mind of God and this put him ahead of all things created and placed him in the position of dominion and authority on earth. Adam was created to be the first king to rule the world. His throne and seat of power was in the garden of Eden. All things created were to be under his rule not the reverse. There is no limit or duration to his reign, it was to be an everlasting reign. Gen1: 28-30

"The living spirit of God transfers through his breath into Adam, makes him see things like God, reason like God and makes him a supernatural being like God. Through the SPIRIT he was able to see into the mind of God and this put him ahead of all things created and placed him in the position of dominion. Adam was created to be the first king to rule the world. His throne and seat of power was in the garden of Eden. All things created were to be under his rule not the reverse. There is no limit or duration to his reign it was to be an everlasting reign. "

Gen 1 : 28-30NKJV

"everything that has life." And that is what happened."

Gen 1:28-30 NLT

The original man from God's plan was designed to be like God or better put a lower god reigning here on earth and maximizing his potentials.

"I have said, <u>you are gods</u>; and all of you are children of the most High"

Ps 82:6 NKJV

There is nothing created by God who was expected to exact its rule over man but rather man ruling over them and exploring them for his benefits. This kind of state is what we see in the monarch around the world. All their subjects respect, protect, obey them. The king is all important in the society, as all their subjects do the work and they walk into the harvest of their labor. Jesus make reference to this kind of state after he called the disciple.

"I sent you to harvest what you have not worked for. others have worked and you have adopted their work as your own"

John4:38 ISV

This original man nature, character and lifestyle designed by God which was meant to be transfer from generation to generations. The animals in the forest, fishes in ocean, birds in the sky never sow nor reap, but their foods come as at when needed. Poverty, lack, pains, sorrowing and any other things like them were never in the program of God for man. A king has all things at his reach and does not lack anything at all. The original man was designed to be king or god on earth. That was the mind of God before He made man.

This reigning grace and the kingship rule in God's mind for man was also expressed when angel Gabriel came to announce the birth of the second Jesus Christ who is the second Adam.

"He shall be great and shall be called the son of the Highest: and the Lord God shall give him. The throne of his father David; and he shall reign over the house of Jacob. forever and of his kingdom there shall be no end" Lk1:32-33 NKJV

This pronouncement by angel Gabriel express the mind of God for the man created because Jesus came as a man. He was to REIGN and RULE as king and to be a great being in all capacity. If there is anything called destiny, man was destined by God to be a great king here on earth irrespective of his birth. Jesus had an humble birth, yet he became great. You don't need to be born physically into wealth or a royal family before you become great. According to God's program for man, you are destined for greatness.

God destined man to be king, priest and one who can reason with Him at all levels. Better than angel who were created to be servant to God and man.

"Therefore, angels are only servants—spirits sent to care for people who will inherit salvation."

Heb 1:14NLT

"All the angels are spirits who serve God and are sent to help those who will receive salvation."

Heb 1:14 Easy-to-Read Version

"What are the angels, then? They are spirits who serve God and are sent by him to help those who are to receive salvation."

Heb 1:14 TEV

The above scriptures are to warn those who see angels as lord and are worshiping them. True Angels of God will never receive worship from man. Those worship Angels are indirectly worshipping demons unknowingly. So in God's program, Angels are to serve Him and man.

God puts His spirit in man to enable man discharge his responsibilities correctly. When you live a spirit filled life, and you will experience this. All men and women possesses the spirit of God either great or small, rich or poor. We all have the spirt of God and by that spirit we know all things and the mind of God.

"And has made us unto our God KING and PRIEST; and we shall REIGN on the EARTH"

Rev3:10 KJV

"Come now; and let us reason together, says The Lord...."

Isa1:18 KJV

These scriptures explain the mind of God for the man. He wants man to reign and also to be someone He could reason with. Can you imagine how God place the original in a lofty position. His lofty position draw the attention of a being who lost his own golden position to pride in heaven. Lucifer or Satan the leader of all Angels of God in heaven. Some Angels even joined in a plot against God.

Man, lost his place in destiny to Satan at the garden of Eden when he ate the forbidden fruit. The nature, abilities and potentials of God was never removed from him but became hidden as a result of disobedient (sin). Sin brought a change in that system and curse upon the earth for man.

"And unto Adam he said, because thou hast hearkened unto the voice of thy wife, and hast eaten of the tree, of which I commended thee, saying, thou shalt not eat of it: CURSE is the GROUND for thy sake; in sorrow shalt thou eat of it all the days of thy life; Thorns also and thistle shall it bring forth to the; and thou shalt eat the herb of the field; in the sweat of thy face shalt thou eat bread, till thou return unto the ground; for out of it was thou taken; for dust, thou art, and unto dust shall thou return"

Gen3:17-19 KJV

Sin kills and blocks joy, love, peace, glory, honor and prosperity man has in the garden of Eden. All the splendor was lost totally. Sin then opens man to all evil and all adverse state of life not as God wish it for man but as Satan wish. He never wishes man to manifest in his full potentials. This he did to man so that he will see God as the evil and wicked one who does not show mercy to anyone who offends him. Take note of the above statement of God, he never cursed man he said *"curse be the ground for your sake"*. The gift and blessings of God is without repentance. All the abilities, potentials are still there for us to be a valuable man on earth. The original man was a great man with value on earth not cursed but blessed and so his sons are supposed to be great with value exploring the earth and using it to his advantage. He was also a companion of God in creation a he invented name. We are to join in invention and add value to the created earth thereby making a worth living place.

CHAPTER TWO

DIMENSIONS OF SIN

"Shew us thy mercy, O Lord, and grant us thy salvation."

Ps 85:7 KJV

*"Also to You, O Lord, belongs mercy; For You render
to each one according to his work.*

Ps 62:12 NKJV

*"O satisfy us early with thy mercy; that we may rejoice
and be glad all our days."*

Ps 90:14 KJV

DIMENSIONS OF SIN

Sin was into the world through Satan who made the wife of the original disobeyed God to turned them against God. The purpose of this is to curse a disharmony between man and God and to make man dead to his true potentials and abilities. The trick of his sin come in three dimension which he used to conquer man. Many mighty men and women has been slayed by one of these dimensions and their destiny destroyed. Why many lost their lives half way without fulfilling their God given purpose.

The target of sin as a tool in the hand of the Devil is to make you go against God and thereby cause an enmity between you and God. This will make you to be in agreement with him and become his servant rather than being a king and god on as God intended for you. He was once with God with great potentials, power, glory and capacity. He knew what you stand to gain so he does everything possible to prevent you from manifesting the grace of God in you. Sin brings total separation from God and make your abilities dead as we can see in the life of Samson when he disobeyed God in chosen to be with a strange woman. That disobedience brought an end to his life and the abilities, power and potentials in him. His value disappears. King Saul once prophesy and people wonder if Saul has become a prophet, but when sin entered his life that grace disappear. Sin is a great killer of dreams and potentials. It will reduce your value to nothing but zero and make impossible for you to realize who you are and what you possess.

DECEPTIVE DIMENSION

The deceptive dimension trips man so easily. The devil uses this deceptive power or dimension to win Adam and collect all his rights. Most mighty men from the Bible time till our present day are falling to this trick of sin and losing their rightful possession.

"For God, do know that in the day you eat thereof, then your eyes shall be opened, and ye shall be as gods knowing good and evil"

Gen 3:5 KJV

These were the deceptive words spoken to Eve that makes them loss their position. Devil came with deceptive words to enticed us so we can follow his ways. James said;

"every man is tempted when he is drawn away by his lost and enticed" *James 1:14.*

There is power in deception and there is also a spirit (demon) of deception. No wonder the writer of Hebrew exhort believers thus:

"But exhort one another daily, while it is called today least any of you be hardened through the deceitfulness of sin"

Heb 3:134 KJV

Deceit is a strong tool in the hand of Satan, which he uses in overcoming believers and everyman on earth. To prevent them from manifesting the potential in them. We must watch daily to overcome sin or devil when he comes knocking the door of your heart. If you open the door, he will come in but if you refuse, he remains locked out completely and you will be in-charge of your heart.

PLEASURE DIMENSION

There is a temporary pleasure that sin give that takes away our thought pattern and one is carried away by that for a second. If we consider any of these sins; fornication, adultery, lie, disobedient, envy or jealousy. Every one of them has temporary pleasures which goes with it and it's for a very short season. It does not last.

"And when the woman SAW that the tree was good for food, and that it was PLEASANT to the eyes, and a tree to be DESIRED to make one wise, she took of the fruit thereof and did eat, and gave also unto her husband with her; and he did eat"

Gen 3:6 KJV

The physical look of the fruit took the attention of Eve. Satan saw the right time to strike with the sting of sin. That is why he is serpent, he wait for the right time to sting. Never you get carried away with what you see, God might not be there. It could be sin. Achan got carried away with the appearance of the gold he saw and got killed with his family. He was consumed with the wealth and not the instructions of God for them as touching the good of the Philistines.

"When SAW among the spoils o goodly Babylonish garment, and two hundred shekels of silver, and a wedge of gold of fifty shekels' weight, then I coveted them, and took them; and, behold, they are hiding in the earth in the midst of my tent, and the silver under it"

Josh7:21 KJV

David lost most of his sons for the pleasure of sin. When kings go to battle, he was at home, which wasn't wrong. He had able war lords to handle any battle and more so he was becoming old. But what he did brought sword into his home. Sin brought the punishment of God upon his life. He saw Bathsheba, he couldn't take his eyes away. The pleasure of sin for some seconds consumed him and he lost his sense. Went after her and enjoy the pleasure of sin and lost at the end.

"And it came to pass in an eveningtide, that David arose from off his bed, and walked upon the roof of the king's house: and from there he SAW a woman washing herself; and the woman was very BEAUTIFUL to look upon"

2Sam11:2 KJV

In David's right senses he wouldn't have done anything of suchs. The power of the sin's pleasure dimension is swift. The short enjoyment of it is like honey when you give your heart to it but stings like scorpion. We the good children of God must come to the point Moses came when he was in Pharaoh's palace and we will always overcome it when it comes.

"By faith Moses, when he was come of year, refused to be called the son of Pharaoh's daughter; choosing rather to suffer affliction with the people of God, than to enjoy the pleasure of SIN for a season"

Heb11:24-25 KJV

The pleasure of sin you choose to enjoy today could be the destruction of your destiny. Moses forsake the pleasure of today to secure his tomorrow. Joseph equally flee when Satan came with room for him to enjoy the pleasure of sin. He said <u>"How can I do this and sin against God."</u> He didn't say to sin against his father or his master, he knew that it will take away his glory and disconnect him from his true nature and God. Sin is a glory snatcher, kill your potential and reduce your value to nothing. Give up that pleasure and you will secure your destiny.

DESTRUCTIVE DIMENSION

Devil and sin seek daily to destroy man. Apostle John said the Devil came to steal, kill and to destroy. Once man give in to the deceptive and pleasure of sin, it leads to death.

"For dust, thou art, and unto dust shall thou return. Therefore, the Lord God sent him (man) forth from the garden of Eden to till the ground from whence he taken. So, he drove out the man; and he placed at the east of the garden of Eden, cherubim and a flaming sword which turned every way to keep the way of the tree of life"

Gen 3:19b,22-23 KJV

No matter how good a sin may look, it leads to death. The man created became dead to his godly nature and die spiritually. This death was never in God's plan, program and purpose for him. What you see on earth today is the end result of sin. The truth is that sin kills your true identity and makes you a vain (empty) man. Living as if you don't have anything to offer on earth. You're dead to your true nature and potentials.

"When that desire becomes pregnant, it gives birth to sin; and when that sin grows up, it gives birth to DEATH"

James 1:15 ISV,

"There is a pathway that seems right to a man, but in the end it's a road to DEATH."
Pro 14:12 ISV

That godly nature in original man that enables him to know the mind of God dies. The abilities, wisdom, knowledge of God dies and his value reduced to nothing. Man, that was intended to rule, reign and subdue the earth, now serve the other things created by God. Man, even bow down in worship to stones, wood and animal such as elephants, crocodiles, snakes and many others calling them god. What a great loss of identity and value. We changed our lofty position for servant-hood to the Devil. What a pity and shame. A king becoming a servant. There are many communities where they serve snakes, water, sun, moon, etc. Remember the Israelites were dancing to the golden calf idol when Moses went for the first forty days to be with God to collect the ten commandment. Man lost his sense of reasoning totally because of sin and lost his value.

When you allow sin in your life this way similar thing also happen to you. You will think you are the most sensible person not knowing you are the greatest fool. Running away from sin is the beginning of wisdom and restoration of your identity, glory, power, beauty and potentials. Your value will change drastically and you will become a significant person in your society.

My final word for everyone reading this piece is that they should run from all appearance of sin. Satan come these three ways. He used it against Jesus Christ after his fasting before he started his ministry. Apostle John make it clear for us to understand it so as to know how to handle them in his writing to the church.

"Do not love this world nor the things it offers you, for when you love the world, you do not have the love of the Father in you. For the world offers only a craving for physical pleasure, a craving for everything we see, and pride in our achievements and possessions. These are not from the Father, but are from this world. And this world is fading away, along with everything that people crave. But anyone who does what pleases God will live forever."

1 John 2:15-17 NLT

He made it clear that the world (Satan) offers to us bodily pleasure which is lust of the flesh, desire for what we can see which is the lust of eyes and pride in our achievements and possessions which is the pride of life. He tried it of Jesus and failed. That shows that we can overcome all of these tricks when he bring them our way. He is what the preacher also said and what we should do.

"My son, those who love to do wrong will try to trick you. Don't listen to them. My son, don't follow them. Don't even take the first step along that path. They run to do something evil,…"

Prov 1:11, 15,16 Easy-to-Read Version

We are to handle sin and his tricks these way:

Never listen to their words. Use God's written words to counter their words as Jesus Christ did to Satan "it is written" Mtt4: 4-10

Don't follow them or their ways. Command him to get away from you as Jesus Christ did. " Get away Satan it is written…" Mtt4: 10

Don't take the first step along their path. Remember what the book of Provaebs says;

"There is a path before each person that seems right, but it ends in death."

Prov14:12

Do what Joseph did run away from the. That is to separate from them. Gen39:12

This way it will be difficult for the Devil to take what belong to you and you will assume you role and full potential on earth and king and priest on earth. You're designed to rule and reign as men and women of great value.

CHAPTER THREE

INGREDIENTS OF VALUE

"Innovation distinguishes between a leader and follower"

Steve Jobs, Apple co-founder

*" The must pathetic person on earth is the one
who has sight but no vision?*

Helen Keller

*"Understand that you can live the life of your dreams,
don't settle for a life of mediocrity"*

ATGW

*"Nothing in life is to be feared, it is only to be understood. Now
is the time to understand more, so that we may fear less"*

Marie Curie

INGREDIENTS OF VALUE

The ingredients you put together determine the quality or value of the cake. For a caterer to have a good looking cake, there are ingredients that must be put in place for it to be eatable presented in parties. Our life requires some necessary ingredients to make valuable to the people we live with and in the society. Let us examine each of this values and how they can add color or beatify to our lives and help recreate the world.

KNOWLEDGE

Knowledge is seen as one of the common element that many beliefs they have but yet they lack it totally. Knowledge is defined as having the right information or fact on how a certain task should be done. In a simple way knowing something. Knowledge is the success key that puts you in charge and makes you do things the right way. A man without knowledge is a novice and foolish.

The Bible says this about what God says in the book of Hosea:
"My people are destroyed for lack of knowledge. Because you have rejected knowledge, ..."

Hos 4:6 NKJV

From the able passage, lack of knowledge destroy. It doesn't matter what kind of business you are involved in, it will fall if you fail to seek more knowledge of that business. The second part is that people rejects knowledge. Knowledge doesn't jump at people but must be consciously acquired. There is someone who have more knowledge than what you have now about your business. Ability to humble yourself to learn from him or her will change your value. Once you fail to do this, you've position yourself and business at the angle where you will attract failure. Frustration in business, work or ministry comes when one doesn't have knowledge of what next to do. Many know what to do that is why they stared very well but gets to a point where they are confused and doesn't know what next should be done. That is where the problem come and they end up failing.

Go for additional knowledge and your value and that of that business will increase. God is a God of knowledge. Can you imagine the depth of His knowledge? He knows all the animals and human beings on earth by name and character. He knows the number of hairs on their head and body. He know the number of stones of earth and their weight.

"With his knowledge, he made springs flow into the rivers and the clouds drop rain on the earth"   *Pro3:20LT*

The whole earth is surrounded by water, beneath is water and above is water (cloud). The small portion of land hasn't been overrun by these water bodies. This can only be by knowledge. The way God has the full knowledge of how to work, so man must have the full knowledge of his or her profession. Knowledge is required in all areas of life, where it's lacking, it leads to failure or total frustration. Knowledge (information) is the greatest asset anyone can possess. Go for more knowledge in your field of life and you will increase your value. New knowledge is required of us also in our field, don't be satisfied with what you have, seek new knowledge and skills daily and you will become master of your field. This will make your value to increase and you will be respected.

"The labor of fools wearies them, for they do not even know how to go to the city!"

Ecc10:15NKJV

When you possess knowledge, it will build you up, guide you, enrich your life, correct and direct you, puts you ahead of others, empowers and increases you more and more on your chosen path of life. Your value changes significantly when you increase your knowledge.

WISDOM

Wisdom is the another ingredient or element that guarantees increase of our value. Wisdom is defined by the American comprehensive dictionary as: common sense or possessing sense of good right judgement. Ability to discern or judge what is true. If simple put right application of acquired knowledge. The right way of using those acquired knowledge is wisdom.

"Wisdom is the principal thing: therefore, get wisdom get understanding. Exalt her and she shall promote thee, she shall bring thee to honor, when thou dost embrace her"

Pro4:7-8 KJV

From the above passage, we must note that "she" was used for wisdom because she can reproduce herself. Whatever that can reproduce has life. Wisdom makes the acquired knowledge in you productive. Unproductive knowledge is a waste to the person who acquired it. How many of your acquitted knowledge are producing for you? Therefore wisdom is the principal thing in life as said in the above passage. Knowing what to do is good but knowing how to apply these knowledge is the best. God makes use of it in the course of creation at the beginning of life. This shows how important wisdom is among all things existing in God. Wisdom was with God at creation.

"The Lord brought me forth as the first of his works, before his deeds of old" Pro8:22 NIV

"The Lord by wisdom hath founded the earth…" Pro3:19a KJV

"By wisdom the Lord laid the earth's foundations" Pro3:19aNIV

"The Lord made the earth using his wisdom" Pro3:19LT

The wonders of creation in Genesis was made possible by the power of wisdom. When we look carefully into the creatures we can perfectly see the power of wisdom at work. No animal looks alike no matter how closely related they are. There is always a line of different in identical twice. This is possible because God is the master of wisdom.

Beloved, if God couldn't do without wisdom you need wisdom to excel in any venture. You need it to increase your value or quality in life. Every one created by God who carries God's spirit should possess wisdom. The question we need to ask ourselves is; Do all possess wisdom? Do all have common sense? Do all have right sense of judgement? The answer to all of these is, NO. We need to seek wisdom like a lost jewel.

We can gain the following benefits and more when we possess wisdom: more market, increase in financial net worth, precious and happier life, riches, honor, pleasantness, peace, glory and grace. How can one possess these qualities and his / her value will not increase? Go for wisdom it will increase your value or quality in whatever you do. The designing of the world and its decorations was made possible with the help of wisdom. The qualities you see on products around is made possible by the right application of wisdom by the producer. The various inventions by different inventors in technology, electronics, electrical, mechanicals etc. are products of wisdom. As born again child of God, Christ is your wisdom. Having Christ is possessing the wisdom of God and the power of God we've lost.

"But Christ is the power of God and the wisdom of God to those people God has called Jews and Greeks"

1Cor1:24LT

UNDERSTANDING

Understanding is ability to comprehend something or the ability to have mental grasp of a content, subject or an action. When you have the right understanding of any content it will lead to establishment in life. One must understand why you're doing what you're doing. The reason why many fail is because they never understood why they are where they are or why they are doing what they are doing. This is why many fail life.

"The Lord by wisdom hath founded the earth by understanding has he established heavens"

Pro3:19b KJV

"If you want to build a tower, you first sit down and decide how much It will cost, to see if you have enough money to finish the job"

Lk14:28LT

"First, finish your outside work and prepare your field. After that, you Can build

your house"

Pr o24:27LT

It's expected of a wise master builder to have a full understanding of what he intends to build before he embark on the work. If he doesn't he will fail. Do you sit back to always think on what you intend doing or do you set out on that project blindly? Employ understanding more than before, then you will experience establishment like God. God established the heavens by understanding. Heavens streets are made of gold as recorded in the book of Revelation. Understanding brings establishment and it's a proof that you are a living being. Do you want to be establish in your life's carrier? Go for understanding on that field.

The Bible says this about one who strays away from the path of understanding..

"A man who wanders from the way of understanding will rest in the

assembly of the dead."

Prov 21:16 NKJV

"The person who strays from common sense will end up in the company of the dead."

Prov 21:16 NLT

So a man without understanding is a dead man. Understanding keeps, you alive and makes you relevant at your workplace, church, home and any other place you may find yourself. If understanding is life it then means it can grow. This way your company can grow, your home changes, you can get promoted, your wealth can increase, new invention can come up, new model of cars can be built, office and home appliances can come out yearly and the face of our cities, towns and villages can changing. Whatever understanding added to you is to change your value. If any company decide not to seek understanding on how to change their product, they will soon be out of business. The face of major cities of the world that is changing through perfect understanding in making them to attract new tourist every day. This constant changes is making Dubai, Shanghai, Hong Kong, Sydney and many other new cities of the world to grow rapidly. Understanding will change your face. Give you rapid promotion above all your equals. And soon you can become their boss. Your value changes drastically once understanding find its way into your life.

Wisdom and understanding is an undisputable ingredients that can change your value overnight. Please go for it with all your strength and your value or net worth will increase. The perception of people about you will change. The value of Daniel and his friends changed at the end of their schooling in Babylon when they manifested undisputable wisdom more than the wise men of the land. They were promoted and became one of the rulers of the land. Your value will also change in that office or establishment if you improve on the level of the wisdom and understanding in carrying out your work.

"As for these four young men, God gave them knowledge and skill in all literature and wisdom; and Daniel had understanding in all visions and dreams…… And in all matters of wisdom and understanding about which the king examined them, he found them ten times better than all the magicians and astrologers who were in all his realm."

Dan 1:17,20NKJV

Daniel and his friends were promoted above all the wise men in Babylon because they manifested undeniable wisdom and understanding in all areas for which they were questioned. Similar thing also happened to Joseph in Egypt when he gave a counsel to Pharaoh on how best he can handle the situation coming ahead of them. The king said "can we find a man like this who have the spirit of God and possibly full of wisdom and understanding in this land? He was appointed as the second in command to the king above all governors, princes and leaders of Egypt. Wow! Some from prison. That is what these ingredient can change someone's value, net worth, life and position overnight.

HOW UNDERSTANDING WORKS

1)   **Concentration:** For anyone to have perfect understanding of issues or content, you must concentrate very well. Your level of concentrations must be deep. You must learn to be alone with

God and think on the project deeply. Then divine ideas flow smoothly. To concentrate you need to control your thought and be sure it concentrate only on the issue you are analyzing or issue you want resolved. Our intellectual mind functions whenever you concentrate and perfect understanding comes. Noise or been in noisy place distract or hinders our concentration.

2) **Focus**: Anyone that loses focus easily can never comprehend. You must be focused and pay attention at all time for your understanding level to increase. Focus on one issue at a time. Focusing on many issue will lead to confusion and get you nothing.

3) **Patience:** Patience is process of been calm in the spirit. Patience is one of the keys that opens door to understanding. Anyone who is always in hurry to get things done without proper understanding of that issue can never get things done correctly. It increases our level of thinking. It's not slowness or slackness. There is strength in patience. It adds more value to you in the end. It makes you gather strength as you go along.

4) **Power of Reason:** Abilities to reason out issues correctly and rightly. This is seeing issues from different sides or perspectives. Anyone who can do this will have full understanding of whatever they are focusing on or analyzing. Once they are able to reason things out correctly, their value can never remain the same. Most people jump at things without thinking. Not many people think. What we call common sense isn't common. Ability to reason is rare, only few people uses this power within them. Those are the few who are successful around us. While others are on looker who act on what those few thinks.

Understanding is paramount to our existence for our value to increase. If you want the qualities of that business, family, work, and ministry to increase, then work on your level of understanding. Make use of it as God did and you will be perfectly established.

DETERMINATION

Determination is an act of been firm on a purpose. You make a decision and you stick to it without wavering. It can be put in a simple way as an act of making up ones' mind to achieve a fixed task or purpose. Determination is stability in your purpose. You must be stable, firm, focus and have a firm purpose to achieve greatness. Anyone who is unstable and not firm in his decision can never increase in his or her value. James said an unstable man is like a wave on the sea and cannot get anything done in life or get anything from God. It takes determination on the side of David to defeat Goliath who happens to be the champion of Philistine and has been fighting for many years. David has all limitations, a youth, a civilian, untrained solder but he employed the power of determination. A determined person is confidence that he or she can do all things. David was so determine to bring him down like he did to the bear and the lion when they came to attack the flocks of his father. Determination build courage in you and give birth to good result.

"Therefore, my beloved brethren, be ye steadfast, unmovable, always abounding in the work of the Lord, for as much as ye know that your labour is not in vain in the Lord"

1Cor15:58 KJV

David value changed completely after this event as a result of firm determination within him to confront the champion. He was praised more than the king and other mighty solders. Anybody's value can change if you can have a firm decision on issues in your life, career, business, workplace or any areas of life.

CREATIVITY

Creativity is the ability to create or invent new for the use of everyone. Every event or items in life were created by someone. The product of creativity is inventions which comes out of our mind. The original man created by God has the creative ability like God, because we have his spirit within us which enables us to do what God did. Powerful thinking gives birth to powerful creativity. We all have the mind of Christ to create and understand if we subject our mind to critical thinking. You are a potential inventor if you can look within you.

"What we have received is not the spirit of the world, but the Spirit who is from God, so that we may understand what God has freely given us."

1Cor2:12NIV

Our brain is a computer without limit. It's from the Lord and the hard ware capacity is big enough to contain any information. While the memory can be stretched to endless limit. It can be developed, improved, redundant., unproductive, resourceful, un-resourceful, format and reset. Creative thinking and powerful understanding mind adds color to anyone's life. Understanding with creative thinking works hand in hand. Statistics shows that about ninety percent of people in the world have redundant creative mind while only ten has active creative mind. That is why there are only few wealthy or successful people on earth. These creative people were inventors, company owners, leaders at all levels and other areas filled with different ideas and concepts that defines the society. Ability to use their creative mind put wealth and riches on the lap. Jacob employed the power of his creative mind with the help of the spirit of God to increase his net worth. He improvised a stick that an ordinary mind can't imagine.

"And the man increases exceedingly and had much cattle, and maidservants and menservants and camels and assets"

Gen30:43 KJV

When we consider the various inventors, they employed the power of their creative thinking ability. Today they are men to be reckon with in the society. Their names live on years after their death. If you seek to increase your net worth or value, the power of creativity must be put to work. This power lays unused within you waiting for exploration. God made use of this power during creation and the result was that everything created was very good.

"God saw all that he made, and it was very good...."

Gen1:31a NIV

Gen1:3-25, shows us in details what God created and how they were created. The beauty of creation can be seen there. If you have to increase your value or net worth you must put to work the creative abilities within you from today. You will be amazed with the result of your value when you explore the power of your imagination. Whatever you can think, you can achieve if you believe it's possible and your value will change significantly.

"Now unto him that is able to do exceeding abundantly above all that we ask or think, according to the power at work in us"

Eph3:20 KJV

The power within you is the power of your imagination. God made you in his image at creation, the value we give God is very high because of the amazing things He created or invented from His imagination. Many people are using their imaginations to do amazing things like God and their value are changing daily. Just take a little minute and reflect on things invented by someone like you. Such as, cars, airplane, rocket, computer, telephone, refrigerator, various home and office appliances, men going to the space and moon, medical equipment, skyscrapers, flying cars etc. Government policies are initiated by individual persons in government. Their ideas and concepts has helped to shape the society and make it a worthy place to live. The Emirate of Dubai have turned desert to a flourishing place to behold by the global world by putting their initiatives and creative mind to work. They created a city from desert improve on what God did at creation.

Different men and women put their creative mind to work and they came up with them. Most of them has engrave their names on the world. They have the same birth like you and even worst family background. They changed their value and net worth by putting their creative abilities to work. Enough of waiting for one uncle, aunty or fathers' wealth, put what you have within you to work and your value will change.

COURAGEOUS

Courageous is defined as a state of being confident not afraid or easily intimidated by any form of fear. This will engineer you to maintain a high level of achieving your dream, vision or desired goal. There may be tendency of frustrations, defeats or failure on the way, but you choose to stand strong seeing only victory, success and celebration at the end of the pains. Those negative tendencies will fade away and your desired result will manifest.

God charged Joshua to be strong and courageous because he was going to fight the giants and if he gives in to the fear of them or their numbers he will lose. Courage will drive you to victory in the midst of oppositions.

"Have not I commanded thee? Be strong and of a good courage; be not afraid, neither be thou dismayed: for the Lord thy God is with thee whithersoever thou goest."

Josh 1:9KJV

Anyone seeking for success and great achievement needs to be courageous like Joshua. Joshua overcame all the giants on his way and took over their land and territories. There are many oppositions like these giants and competitors in your line of business who are ready to do anything to push you out so that they will be the only one. Your co-workers or boss might be giving you attitude in that office so you can make mistake and be fired, never give in to any of their moves, be strong and be courageous to face them and shame will cover them when you become their boss. Then your value and your net worth has changed and increased which is your outmost dream.

DILIGENCE

This is a state or quality of been a hard worker, determined, perseverance and consistent in getting things done. This includes you having an industrious spirit that focus and concentrate on achieving a desired goal or result.

"He who has a slack hand becomes poor, But the hand of the diligent makes rich"

Prov 10:4NKJV

"The plans of the diligent lead surely to plenty, but those of everyone who is hasty, surely to poverty."

Prov 21:5NKJV

"Seest thou a man diligent in his business? he shall stand before kings; he shall not stand before mean men."

Prov 22:29KJV

The scriptures above are very clear, a diligent person must rule, become rich, his or her plans will lead him or her to the land of plenty. He or she has nothing to do with the poor but the rich will be his or her companions. The diligence people are the rulers and movers of the world. Hard work doesn't kill or make you sick as many thinks or belief, it's laziness that kill easily. A diligent person is skillful in his or her business and ready to go extra miles to get things done. Success, wealth, victory and prosperity sticks to such people. Diligence will surely make you shine like star to people around you. Examine the big shorts around you, you will discover that they are diligent workers. Have you ever seen them in club houses or in an uncompromising way lazing around when they supposed to be at work? They only do that when they are They are too busy for such a thing. If you want to increase your value or net worth, be diligent in any task given to you without complaining.

INNOVATION

Innovation is an act or a state of introducing a new idea, product, or style into a system to change the course of things. This process of doing something new different from what is obtainable in the environment is to cause a revolution in the system. The introduction of personal computer into the system of business has changed the world from using typewriter. Olympia and IBM typewriters has gone into extinction. The children of this generation don't know those name.

Facebook and WhatsApp has also changed the face of our social media. Those who introduced them into the system of media are good innovators and their value has changed thereby increasing their net worth.

Whatever idea that comes into your mind that looks un-achievable could be an idea to turn your life or business around and if you throw it away another person will pick it up. Just carefully examine all fields you will discover those men who have causes revolutions within it are never forgotten. Their names and works lives on for many years after they've gone out of this world. That is what am saying. Generations unborn will always know any innovative man or woman. Ortega the owner of Zara textile company in Italy introduce a system of marketing and supply chain that only him understood. People called his style of supply chain a crazy one, today he is one of the richest people of the world. Ortega believe his idea and he stuck to it, he never copies or follow the conventional way of supply chain. His value and net worth has been increasing year after year. He is one of the wealthy giants of the world today. Believe in those ideas no matter how illogical it may look it will change your value and net worth when it becomes generally acceptable by everyone.

DEDICATION

Dedication is defined as a state of been committed to a particular course of action or task accomplish a purpose or a desired result. Been committed will always lead you to great success in your career or any area you may be called upon to work. Doing work with levity and laxity is to reduce your value. For example if a task is given to you and it takes a whole day for to accomplish it while your other colleague finished and submitted within few hour.

The way and manner people use the social media these days has reduced their level of dedication. Workers leave work and students also leave their books to chatting and responding to mails with hope of doing their work later. All of these actions reduces their commitment level. If people can be committed to their carriers or studies the way and manner they are dedicated to their phones, their values would have changed. Their actions has made Mark Zuckerberg one of the richest persons in the world. His value and net worth has grown rapidly over the years. Your intensity of dedication to social media should be reduced and be more dedicated to your visions and dreams to change your value and increase your net worth. You can also create a product that will draw people and money like the owners of those social media and before you know it you're among the valuable people in the society.

CONSISTENCE

Consistence is the ability to remain at a particular pattern or way of doing things or the state of doing something over and over without given up or getting tired. People get tired when they start doing the same thing over and over. A lot of people give up and move to something else when they can't see quick result in that line of work, or ministry they are engaged in. When they see someone else succeeding in that line latter they say I've do that business before. But you chicken out. Moving from one business to another without a set goal is inconsistency and confusing of mind. Focus on one business and don't stop it until you succeed, that is the power of consistency. Once you've achieved your dream in that line of business or ministry and its doing well, you can move to another one. This is diversification or having streams of business.

Once you have an inspiration to do something, stick to it. There is a glory waiting for you in that line. It doesn't matter how long it takes you to succeed, stay on and be focus with it you will soon shine. If Thomas Edison had giving up that idea of light, another person would have invented it and the glory won't be for him. "I tried" is not a language of a successful person. But their language is "I got it" "I achieved it". To achieve anything, you need the power of consistency. Ortega stuck to his system and today he is swimming in money.

All these ingredients must find expression in your life if you are to change your value and thereby increase your net worth.

CHAPTER FOUR

VALUED LIVES ARE RELEVANT

"Increase your value as each day goes by to increase your value and net worth"

Oluwafemi Dennis

"learn to work hard on yourself than your job. if you work on your job, you make a living but if you work hard on yourself, you will make a fortune"

Jim Rohn

"Your core values are the deeply held beliefs that authentically describe your soul"

John Maxwell

"Good values are like a magnet they attract good people"

John Wooden

"Your value determines your acceptance in the society and net worth."

Oluwafemi Dennis Ojo

VALUED LIVES ARE RELEVANT

Salt is relevant in cooking and its value is great in making your food tasty. There is nothing that is relevant in the entire world of cookery as salt and there is no nation where it's not recognized. Jesus compares our life with salt when delivering one of his sermons on who we are.

"You are the salt of the earth, but if the salt has lost its flavor, with what will it be salted? It is then good for nothing but to be cast out and trodden under the feet of men"

Matt 5:13 NKJV

There is a clear difference between food that has taste and one without taste. The value you give to the one with salt is greater than the other one without salt. That why you can't eat diabetic patients' food. Anyone, who labors to improve himself/herself will become relevant like salt to the earth. God created us to add taste and value to humanity. The same way salt is very important, you are of utmost importance and significance. You are a personality that your world cannot do without. In fact, your family, immediate environment or nation and the world at large will be influenced by you and they will always celebrate you. You are too beautiful and important to be trampled or sidelined in life. If your life is not adding value to people, your level of relevance has gone forever.

Relevance is an act of being important or being needful. It's your level of importance and significance. God created you special because He knows the impact you will make on Earth. You can touch people's lives with the positive impact you make in their lives.

The relevancy of the salt cannot be substitute for any other ingredients. So our lives should be relevant in a way that people we relate with will find it difficult to substitute us for another person. Albert Einstein said "try not to become a man of success, but rather try to become a man of value". He see that we should develop our character as we seek to become successful. This way the true success will emerge. But if you want to be successful without developing your character, you may lose your relevancy.

Many people we meet daily seek ways for them to be successful but to be successful different from been valuable. You can be successful and not be valuable but you can't be valuable without becoming successful. All your attentions should be focused on how to improve your value.

HOW TO INCREASE YOUR RELEVANCY?

1) ACQUIRE NEW SKILL DAILY

If you want to remain in your present position, or you want a new job add value to yourself. This will make you relevant in that office. If value of your contribution in that position is high, you will remain relevant. That will surely lead to more pay and benefits and quick promotion than someone whose value remain unchanged. More confidence and responsibilities will be giving to you. Look for new skills in your field and get expertise. It will make you relevant and your value will change.

2) BE THE MASTER OF YOUR FIELD.

Your goal in life should be to organize your life in a way that you enjoy every bit of life and activities, have a good high standard of living, and you are the master in your line of business or profession. Your profession is an opportunity to contribute to the world around you and this will make more money and honor comes your way, then your relevancy has increase. Masters are always in-charge and others follows. Being a master will make you to be prefer above your co-workers and soon you will become their boss. Being a master makes your boss or superior have more confidence. It brings more responsibilities which will attract more pay and your value in that office increases.

3) IMPROVE YOUR KNOWLEDGE AND EDUCATION.

Don't stop learning or add new knowledge and certificate to whatever you've gotten. Your education, knowledge, skills and experience are investment to improve your value and net worth. Online education or learning has made it possible for us to acquire new certificate to increase our value.

A senior friend was good at his work in a multinational company and the company find it difficult to allow him go for annual leave. The company always buy his leave because of his relevancy. We advised him to go for more certification which he started but couldn't finished it because of laziness. His salary grew so much that the company seek ways to remove him. They look for new people with more certificates than him and with little pay to understudy him. After a while he was asked to go for one week leave. When he returned he access those junior staff, gave them 70% performance. After a year of understudy, the company asked him to go for his annual leave that they can't pay for it again. He did and this new people took charge of the office so well.

A year later he was retired and the new people took over the position and his responsibilities were shared among three persons with little pay. The company gained and he has lost. He wasn't sensitive to the time, and the moves of the company. He couldn't get a new job because he has no certificate to back up the position in his resume. He was out of job forever. Add new certificate to whatever you've gotten to increase your value and you will be relevant in your office.

4) BE ORIGINAL

Be the real person God has created you to be. Don't try to be another person. You're not a photocopy. I've seen many people speaking like their leader or boss. For him to be who you emulate, he developed himself to become who he is. You are special and wonderful the way God created you. Trying to be like another person is to reduce your value. All you need to become great is in you, discover it and develop it and your value will increase. Trying to be someone else makes you look inferior and you are not inferior, you are original and special. Job told his friends he his original and not an inferior in any way to them. "What you know, I also know; I am not inferior to you." Job 13:2 NIV. Always be yourself at all time and seek ways to develop yourself.

5) YOU ARE A PRODUCT

See yourself as product to the world. God sent you here for a purpose. That was why Jesus says you are the salt of the world. To add taste and value to the world. The world is waiting for you to manifest. Whatever you are using today; clothes, shoe, electronic, computer, houses cars, airplane were products of somebody's mind and investment of time to make impact in the world. What are you going to leave behind for the next generation? Whatever you produce is your product to the world and it will surely speak for you. Light will keep speaking for Thomas Edison. I love what Paul said to the Roman Christians it also applies to everyone in the world today.

"For the earnest expectation of the creature waiteth for the manifestation of the sons of God."

Rom 8:19 KJV

The world is waiting for your product to be revealed. Those without values are disappointments to heaven and the world. They are men and women of no value. They are a waste product. Not because they were created that way, they make themselves a waste. Your good ideas are a product to your office. There is a great power within you waiting to be tap. You are placed here on earth to continue God's work of creation. You are produced to produce something for others to use. That is what makes the world to continue and beautiful. You are not to use other people's product without making your own product available for others. If you don't use the ability in you, it goes with you to the grave. Great ideas and visions makes the grave the richest place on earth. Men and women who were designed to turn the world around die daily without realizing who they are or living their full potential.

6) CREATE DAILY DREAM

Have a vision of what to achieve daily, weekly, monthly and yearly. Break your big dream or vision to smaller bits and take actions on them. Living without dream will make you vulnerable to any persons dreams, opinions and suggestions. Daily dreams give you sense of direction and purpose. You will never be a wanderer again. As workers in an office, what is your dream for that position? Dream to grow faster than others. Students have a dream to have the best result and create time to read or search more than others. This act will help you to achieve many task at a time and your life or business will experience significant growth.

7) JOIN VOLUNTEERS

Volunteering makes you showcase your skills and potentials. Your newly acquired potentials will be open for people to see for those working and the unemployed. Many have gotten new jobs through this and have changed their status. Any opportunity of volunteering should be seen as avenue to make yourself relevant. Do it with joy and happiness without complaining. This is also an act of giving your service, time, energy, wisdom, potentials and skills for the benefit of God or others and the reward will surely be bigger than the seed you sown.

8) NETWORKING

Networking is another way to make yourself relevant. Net working with other people opens you to new skills. It also allows you to show case your own skills and potentials. Networking make you meet new people who might be bosses of company or government official looking for new people to hire. When they see your skill, a new office is waiting for you with better pay.

Jim Rohn said "learn to work hard on yourself than your job. If you work on your job, you make a living but if you work hard on yourself, you will make a fortune" Focusing on self-development is the best and it will make your value to increase day by day. The task you are giving today might need new skills to handle. If that skill is not in you, and the company have to get some else to do it, just know you're out of that office. You will always get paid for the value you bring to work. You get little or nothing when you are not valuable.

Value every time that comes your way to contribute positively to increase your value so as to be relevant and make sure you are at your best in everything you do. This way your relevancy will be incomparable and your value will be like salt or a lamp with a big light shining for others to see. Your daily, weekly, monthly and yearly vision should be to increase your value or net worth. This will generate an unseen energy within you that seek opportunity to contribute positively to the world around you. So valuable men and women are people who turn their world around and make themselves relevant for their generation and generations to come.

CHAPTER FIVE

VALUED LIVES IMPACTS THE WORLD

"Before you speak, listen. Before you write, think. Before you spend, earn. Before you invest, investigate. Before you criticize, wait. Before you pray, forgive. Before quit, try. Before you retire, save. Before you die, give."

> *William. A. Ward*

"Only buy something that you'd be perfectly happy to hold if the market shuts down for ten years"

> *Warren Buffett*

"It's not the employer who pays the wages. Employers only handle the money. It's the customer who pays the wages"

> *Henry Ford*

"A man without vision / dream lives by the impressions, opinions and suggestions from various ends, he can't impact the world"

> *Oluwafemi Dennis Ojo*

VALUED LIVES IMPACTS THE WORLD

The world has recorded great men and women who have impacted the it so greatly and have written their names with golden pen on the earth. Their relevancy cannot go without been noticed. The pages of the Bible, history books,

Wikipedia have list of such men and women. They were valuable in their own time and generations after them are celebrating them and their work. The only generation they were never valued are the generations before them. They partner with God in recreating the world and making it a more beautiful place to live than the time of Adam in the garden of Eden.

Some are inventors, philosophers, doctors, engineers, painter, artist, writers, teachers, preachers, leaders of their countries, kings of kingdoms, etc. When you look within your area, the names of such people are written with golden pen. Generations will keep referring to them as great men and women of value who has helped shaped or recreate the world and make it a better place to live.

Let's take a look at the chronicles of such men and women from the bible to the secular world to learn how they've make themselves valuable. Their character traits can be taking in by you and your greatness will surely surpass them.

1) ENOCH
"Enoch walked with God; then he was no more, because God took him away."
Gen 5:24 NIV

"By faith Enoch was taken away so that he did not see death, "and was not found, because God had taken him"; for before he was taken he had this testimony, that he pleased God."

Heb 11:5 NKJV

Nothing was written in the Bible about the activities of this man apart from what James wrote about him and that he walked with God.

"Enoch, the seventh from Adam, prophesied about these men: "See, the Lord is coming with thousands upon thousands of his holy ones to judge everyone, and to convict all the ungodly of all the ungodly acts they have done in the ungodly way, and of all the harsh words ungodly sinners have spoken against him."

Jude 14-15 NIV

This man had prophesy about the coming of Jesus seven generations after Adam. That was great. I called him preacher of righteousness and a prophet in deed. He also pleased God so much that he practically became like God for him to be taken bodily to heaven. Possibly he must have pleased God in his thought, action, words, walks and other areas of his life.

For us to be valuable we must make God first in all areas of our life. Our visions and dream must be in harmony with what God has in mind for us. Do nothing without asking God and make sure you have his approval before going ahead. People may complain, yell or even go away from you, when they later see your success, they will come bowing down for you. It's better to please God like Enoch and our value increase than to please man and remain the same.

2) MEN OF TOWER OF BABEL

Men of Babel keeps amazing me any time I read their story or whenever their story comes to my mind. They were so relevant that the Holy spirit gave their story to Moses when writing the book of Genesis. They were men to be celebrated for their inventions and mind to achieve a set goal. They were visionary men.

"They said to each other, "Come, let's make bricks and bake them thoroughly." They used brick instead of stone, and tar for mortar. Then they said, "Come, let us build ourselves a city, with a tower that reaches to the heavens,"

Gen 11:3-4 NIV

I decided to bring them in here for us to look at the positive side of their life. They invented; burnt bricks, discover bitumen and refine it to tar, built the first sky scraper at a time in the world when there was no technology as we have today. These professions started with them; architecture, Structural/building engineers, bricklayers, carpentry and they must have improvised lift to move materials upwards, they must have done soil analysis to know the best location to site the building (geologist). They had vision, believed it's achievable, saw nothing as limitations and are ready to create anything to achieve their goal, they were united and had team work spirit. They worked as one force with focus on their goal. They must have failed several times without giving up. They must have gone far before God came down to give them different languages and the project stopped. These men failed because of their; selfishness, making name for themselves and planning without God. If you have their positive virtues; have a vision, see no obstacles in life, ready to improvise or create in other to achieve your vision, have never given up spirit and plan with God in mind to be a blessing to the world, then you will stand tall in this world. Have a strong team who believe in your vision or be part of a strong team that is focused. Your value increases if you're a good team player.

3) ABRAHAM

Abraham became great in this world today because he was ready to go into a new location to start a new life with God leading the way. The writer of Hebrew wrote something about him thus;

" By faith Abraham obeyed when he was called to go out to the place which he would receive as an inheritance. And he went out, not knowing where he was going. By faith he dwelt in the land of promise as in a foreign country, dwelling in tents with Isaac and Jacob, the heirs with him of the same promise; for he waited for the city which has foundations, whose builder and maker is God."

Heb 11:8-10NKJV

Leaving our comfort zone is always a difficult task for anyone. Abraham was ready to move as he heard God. He left all his family inheritance of land and houses behind for an unknown place. The passage above says he was looking for a city build by God so he lives in tents and never built a house. What a faith. Today, the whole world is blessed through him as recorded in Gal 3: 8-9 NKJV "In you all the nations shall be blessed." So then those who are of faith are blessed with believing Abraham."

Did he know that his name will become a common name in the world forever? No. He was only obeying God. Dwelling in your comfort zone might be your greatest undo. Be ready like Abraham to explore new areas of business, jobs, carrier and locations for God to make you a great person. Your glory and relevancy might be in that new place. Your unknown generations might be saved through that giant step you're inspired to take, and they will celebrate you for ever taken that step. Your value and net worth will increase. Your name will live on for many years to come like Abraham.

4) MOSES

This man has rare privilege that many people pray and wish they ever have. He happened to be trained in the highest palace of their time. Eat whatever he wants and have the chance of becoming the next king Pharaoh who might rule the then world.

"By faith Moses, when he became of age, refused to be called the son of Pharaoh's daughter, choosing rather to suffer affliction with the people of God than to enjoy the passing pleasures of sin, esteeming the reproach of Christ greater riches than the treasures in Egypt; for he looked to the reward."

Heb 11:24-26 NKJV

He chose to be part of the slave who were servants to the throne than for him to be adore as a crown Prince. That choice changed his destiny for good. Those other children in that palace has been forgotten but Moses name is still living.

Your status is not the determinant of your value but the kind of choice you make. Many people were born by kings, rich men and influential people and they are not as relevant as their fathers. So your birth place or who is your father may not determine your own value. If you don't make the right choice, you will only live on the glory of your father and you will never be remembered for anything.

Most of the mover and shakers of the world today or in the past where born by poor people. But they choose to turn things around in their lives and to increase their value like Moses.

The choice you make may look unimportant today, but because you know where you are going by virtue of the insight you have about decision, you will lead men and women out of poverty to their land of promise or wealth that will affect their generations.

Just imagine those working in; Henry Ford Corporation, Thomas Edison Company, Heinz corporation, McDonald, Walmart, Amazon, Alibaba, and many other companies that started centuries or decades ago. The choice of the founder in those years that look stupid to men and women of that time, is making many rich and employing jobless people in the society today. Thereby putting smiles on people faces. Nations are waiting on them before economic decisions are made. Just go on with that decision and life will be great for you as you increase your value and net worth.

5) DAVID

David was a man whose life is daily inspiring lives from generation to generation. He was a big reference point for other kings that ever lived after him. His leadership was a great one in terms of ruling and reigning over nation. His decision making and approach to issues as they come his way was great. Joab his warlord must have seeing him as stupid and foolish man that day he had opportunity to kill king Saul. His spiritual sensitivity is unquestionable. He saw God's glory several times and function like a prophet alongside his kingship role. He wrote songs, poems and remain the only ordinary person who enters the holy of holies to take the holy bread without him been Levite.

How did he come to this glorious position in Israel and the world? God comes first as his helper as long as David is concern. He said;

"I will look up unto the hills from where come my help, My help come from the Lord who makes the heaven and the earth"

Ps121:1-2 NKJV

"The Lord is my shepherd I shall not want"

Ps23: 1 NKJV

"So David inquired of the Lord, saying, "Shall I pursue this troop? Shall I overtake them?"

1 Sam 30:8 NKJV

"Moreover David said, "The Lord, who delivered me from the paw of the lion and from the paw of the bear, He will deliver me from the hand of this Philistine."

1 Sam 17:37 NKJV

God remain the unquestionable leader, director and guidance of the entire life of David. His confidence in the abilities of God is so great. He does nothing without asking God. The approval of God is all that is important to him. He also desire to experience God daily and be at his presence all the time. He was a good worshiper of God.

"How lovely is your dwelling place, O Lord Almighty! My soul yearns, even faints, for the courts of the Lord; my heart and my flesh cry out for the living God."

Ps 84:1-2 NIV

"Better is one day in your courts than a thousand elsewhere; I would rather be a doorkeeper in the house of my God than dwell in the tents of the wicked."

Ps 84:10NIV

"He who dwells in the secret place of the Most High Shall abide under the shadow of the Almighty."

Ps 91:1NKJV

These psalms can only be written by someone who has gone into the third heaven, saw the glory of God and his awesomeness. How many men in the world has experience God like the way David did? Few. He had good relationship with God. If anyone do what David did, such person will also have similar experience of God's glory. You can't be in the carrier of God glory like David and remain the same. The way and manner David was blessed will also be the way such person will be blessed. David loved God and anything that concerns Him. How do you see God? How do you see the things of God like church, his children around you? Do you easily forgive? Or Do you hold on to offence? Are you ready to give all you have for God's work (church) as David did for the building of the temple in Jerusalem? Or Give to the needy? I mean philanthropist. Are you ready to defend the name of God as David did and kill Goliath? Are you ready to repent in dust and ashes as soon as you fall out of grace like David or you find reason to justify your actions like king Saul and Adam? Are you ready to go extra mile for God? Are you ready to receive abuses for the sake of God? Your right answers to these questions will go long way to help shape your life towards making your life relevant to God and to the world. Once you have the right answer to these questions, your value will never remain the same again. You will discover you are sent on earth to make impact.

God refers to David as a man after his heart. He was a man ready to put his life on the line for the name of God and his course. You can touch David, his wives, children, but don't touch his God and his things, he is ready to die in defending His name. Learn from David's life and your value will never remain the same again and posterity will live to celebrate you for good.

6) APOSTLE PETER

Apostle Peter the leader of the disciples of Jesus Christ is one of the most valued person in history. He is seen today as the first Pope by the Roman Catholic Church Worldwide. He denied his master to his face at the time he would have stand for him. He realized his error asked for the forgiveness of his sin and preached his first ever sermon in the same Jerusalem, he had three thousand souls saved. The same leader before whom he denied his master were in attendance. He made this wonderful statement to them.

"Men of Israel, listen to this: Jesus of Nazareth was a man accredited by God to you by miracles, wonders and signs, which God did among you through him, as you your- selves know. This man was handed over to you by God's set purpose and foreknow- ledge; and you, with the help of wicked men, put him to death by nailing him to the cross. But God raised him from the dead, freeing him from the agony of death, because it was impossible for death to keep its hold on him.

Acts 2:22-24 NIV

After this sermon, the same people who killed Jesus said "men and brethren what shall we do? Peter replied "repent and be baptized and God will forgive all your sins in the name of Jesus Christ".

He later perform many remarkable miracles. His shadow was healing the sick and raising the dead. He touched lives for God and turned many to righteousness. His value changed drastically when he made a U-turn and boldly declared the wonderful works of God.

As you make God your focal point in seen many turn from their wickedness to God, he will load you with great value that will turn your life around for Good. Engage in soul winning and charity.

7) APOSTLE PAUL

Apostle Paul stands out as one of the most valuable men that ever lived in Bible history. His works and the mark he made remain a reference point to everyone. He wrote two third of the book in the New testament, he touched many lives in his lifetime and after his death. He was ready to go to any length for the sake of gospel. He started living this way from the time he was a Pharisee. He was so dedicated to defending what he beliefs that he was ready to kill. Are you dedicated like this to your vision or dream?

I thank God, whom I serve, as my forefathers did, with a clear conscience"

2 Tim 1:3 NIV

"They knew me from the first, if they were willing to testify, that according to the strictest sect of our religion I lived a Pharisee.

Acts 26:5 NKJV

"Indeed, I myself thought I must do many things contrary to the name of Jesus of Nazareth. This I also did in Jerusalem, and many of the saints I shut up in prison, having received authority from the chief priests; and when they were put to death, I cast my vote against them. And I punished them often in every synagogue and compelled them to blaspheme; and being exceedingly enraged against them, I persecuted them even to foreign cities."

Acts 26:9-11 NKJV

Paul was a defender of his religion. You could see that in his statements in the above passages. He was righteous as far the Judaism is concern. When he became a follower of Jesus Christ, he went from place to places saving lives instead of killing them. He was everywhere for Christ. He never complained nor felt sorry for himself but counted himself privileged to be used by God to propel the gospel to the Gentiles. There was no pride in him at any point in time throughout his time of taken the gospel everywhere.

"Who shall separate us from the love of Christ? Shall tribulation, or distress, or persecution, or famine, or nakedness, or peril, or sword? As it is written: "For Your

sake we are killed all day long; We are accounted as sheep for the slaughter." Yet in all these things we are more than conquerors through Him who loved us."

Rom 8:35-36 NKJV

Apostle Paul was a die hearted person. A man full of passion for the good news of Jesus Christ Whatever course he beliefs in, he is good to go and his is ready to die for it. He said nothing can take this course of spreading the gospel away from him. He put his life on the line. With all the challenges he had. If anybody in our days is to go through any of such, he would say let me apply wisdom less I die. Paul was even ready to die. No wonder the world is still celebrating him and his life and work and he is still affecting generations.

If you are to affect lives like Paul, you must have a die heart spirit like him. Nothing on earth will matter to you except the vision in your hand. You must be ready to give all you have for it. Have a strong passion for your vision and that assignment in your hand. Be consume with end result of your vision rather than the obstacles. Pride must never find its way into your life. You must be ready to work at all time. Paul wrote most of his letters from prison. When the enemy thought he has been caged, that was when he made the most impact through writing. Those writings are the scriptures reading today. While writing those letters he was only doing what he felt should be done. Did he write them because he wants it to be part of the Bible? No. He was only building, strengthening, encouraging, edifying the churches, his spiritual children and settling or resolving issues.

You can also learn to put your thought or ideas in writing. You never can tell that may be the key that will announce you to the world. This can be said about Paul; where he couldn't fly, he walked, where he couldn't walk he crew, where he couldn't move his legs or body because of prison, he wrote. Any how his life was influencing people all the way. Be there to do what is right at all time, never you see the obstacles as barriers just keep doing what is right. Keep taking positive steps towards achieving your vision or dream.

Dear reader, please note this that all things are possible for you for as long as you subject your mind to critical thinking. There is always a way out. If Paul had considered his circumstances, he wouldn't have been what he is to the world today. If he says now that he is in prison the people should take care of themselves and he never felt concern about the welfare of the churches he established. That point where you said there is no way, there is a big way the only thing is that you can't calm down and think for you to see it.

Let me bring this examples to make myself clear at this point. I've once be at some points like you are in the past and I do say it's not possible or there is no way out and will be consumed by the chains of the problems around me. There is a way out. Yes. There is always a way out of any hard situations.

Hagar was sent out with her son Ishmael by Abraham with a jar of water and bread in Gen21:8-21. The water got finished in the wilderness of Beersheba and she left her son under a shrub and went away to about a stone throw and started crying because she and the boy are going to die and wasn't ready to witness the death of her son. God sent his angel to her and after their conversation, her eyes was opened and she saw a well. That well has always been there but because she was filled with sorrow and self-pity, she couldn't see it. Do you also know that what you are looking for is not far from you? Wipe your tears away, calm down and God will show you the way out of that situation that so hard. Either in your life, home, office or business.

The Israelites also thought it's was over when they got to the bank of the Red Sea and they suddenly saw Pharaoh with his six hundred chariots apart from the foot solders behind them. The key that divided the Red Sea was Moses rod. That was a ridiculous idea that can only be from God. When such unimaginable idea comes into your mind as the solution to the problem or a way out, don't you argue it and throw them away? Yes we do. Stop doing this as it's the way out given to you by God. Please just go ahead and obey or follow it. At the end you will be the one praising God like Miriam and all the women after crossing the Red Sea and Pharaoh perishing with his armies.

I decided to pick these few people for the sake of this write up. There are so many other people like Samuel, Ruth, Deborah, Hezekiah, Jehoshaphat, Joseph, Elijah, Elisha, Daniel and his friends, Esther, Mordecai, Nehemiah John the Baptist, John the beloved Barnabas etc. The list is just endless in the Bible.

8) JESUS CHRIST

Jesus Christ the Messiah remain the most valued person in all history. No one in the Old, New Testament and after Bible history till today and beyond could be compared to him. He was born in a manger were sheep or animals are kept because his parents did not have their own house in their home town and couldn't afford an inn.

He had a humble birth and not much was recorded of his early life. Jesus went missing for three days at age twelve when he supposed to be playing with other children without a notable visions or dreams. And when he found, he was in the temple discussing with the teachers of the law and asking them questions. His parent asked why did he punished them this way for three days? His reply was;

"And He said to them, "Why did you seek Me? Did you not know that I must be about My Father's business?" ...Then He went down with them and came to Nazareth, and was subject to them,

Luke 2:49, 51 NKJV

At that age he has discovered himself and was with the teachers of the law learning the scriptures. What a focused person. His life mission of redemption made him the most valued person on earth and in heaven. Up to today there is no one like him.

I know that you might say this is Jesus Christ the second person in Trinity. Yes. He is. But while on earth he was a human being like you and me. He left his glory in heaven to become human being.

He came to experience what man complains of to God. From his prayer at the point of leaving this world he made a statement to justify this point that he left his glory in heaven.

"I have brought you glory on earth by completing the work you gave me to do. And now, Father, glorify me in your presence with the glory I had with you before the world began."

John 17:4-5 NIV

The writer of Hebrew also made us understood that Jesus was on earth like any man and was never with the power and glory he had with God. He defeated Satan in human being form. Because he need to be in the form of Adam to redeem man and reconcile them to God.

"For we do not have a high priest who is unable to sympathize with our weaknesses, but we have one who has been tempted in every way, just as we are — yet was without sin."

Heb 4:15 NIV

Jesus Christ went through all the things we complain as limitations or reasons we fall into sin and yet never sin. He never looked at his birth or family status. But focused on his vision and at the end he entered into a glory that his mother and father wouldn't have been able to give him.

Jesus wasn't the only person that discover his destiny early. We have men like; Samuel who started hearing God at eight years, Joseph had a dream of his destiny at a young age, Joash was the youngest king in Judah he became king at seven years 2Chro24:1, Josiah become the king at eight years 2chron34:1. Azariah 2Kgs15:2 become king at sixteen years. They are examples of a good leaders to emulate.

As at the time of writing this book the youngest richest person on earth is only seventeen years old. Bill gate one of the richest men on earth also started very early. Don't justify yourself with that word that you are still small or young. The two friends who started Google search engine started as young men in their room. Mark Zuckerberg CEO of Facebook and WhatsApp started in his room while in school. Is there any different between these people and Jesus Christ who started his ministry at age thirty? No.

What is peculiar with all of these people including Jesus Christ is that they discovered their purpose as early as possible and they put all their energies and ingredients behind it. Their value changed significantly. Learn a great lesson from them. The earlier you start out the better for you. Your net worth will surely increase.

If you are just discovering yourself, don't worry, the day you discover yourself is the day you receive light and your value will start increasing once you can create a vision for yourself. You must determine from that day that things must change no matter the situations and circumstances around you. As you take positive step in this direction, your level must change and you value will surely increase.

EARLY CHRISTIANITY

The early Christianity had many men who brought value to themselves and impacted the world for good. I chose to bring them in for us to see how important it is when you increase your value. Among them are;

1) JOHANNES GUTENBERG

A German goldsmith and black smith who invented the first printer and type writer and produce the first Bible in Latin. Making the Bible to be the first book ever published in history. How can a blacksmith become an engineer and a printer and a publisher? He must have possessed great determination and courage to be able to do that. That single step brought change into the world.

2) MARTIN LUTHER

The Battle-Ax of Reform". A German priest and professor of theology who oppose the teaching of the Roman Catholic Church and set the pace for Pentecostalism in the world. He went again the church leader at the early stage in world history to stand for what was revealed to him even though no one seems to belief, he stood for what God showed him and dead for that course.

3) JOHN WYCLIFFE

The Bible Translator". He translated the Bible from Latin into the first English in 1384 by hand. The whole 80 books of the Bible to be written by hand, wow! That was a great determination from him. Anything is possible. He was a good example to the world to know that determination will always get you good result when you set your heart to achieve any task you're given or set before yourself.

4) WILLIAM TYNDALE

Printed the first English Bible in 1525. He produced the New Testament first his first production was burnt. He was persecuted but escaped to Germany remained hidden until he reproduced it and smuggled it into England. He was on the production of the Old Testament when he was caught and murdered. You have access to the Bible today because of his giant step.

5) MYLES COVERDALE

Coverdale produced the complete Bible 80 books in 1535, ten years after Tyndale was murdered. May be a son of William Tyndale. The complete English Bile own its availability to their his good work.

6) KING JAMES OF ENGLAND

Revised the Myles Coverdale version of the Bible 80 books but officially removed the Apocrypha changed it from traditional English to Shakespearian English and became the most accepted Bible in the world.

After these great people in history, we have great reformers like; John Hus "The Father of Reform:', John Calvin "The Teaching Apostle", John Knox "The Sword Bearer", George Fox "The Liberator of Spirit". Their work pave way for the gospel to spread round world.

The modern day Christianity has been influenced by the works of men like John and Charles Wesley founder of Methodist Church, Charles. G. Finney Bible translator with reference and commentary, E. W. Kenyon, George Whitefield, Jonathan Edward, Billy Graham the great evangelist, Dwight. L. Moody, John. G. Lake, A. A Allen, Lester Sumrall, Oral Robert, Kenneth. E. Hagin, Kathryn Kuhlman, John Osteen etc. The list is endless of great revivalist and evangelist and teacher of the gospel who put their lives on the line for the world to receive the gospel of our Lord Jesus Christ. They can never be forgotten in history.

THE SECULAR WORLD

Let's take look at men who have set the pace for the secular world outside the church circle. These men's work serves as foundation for men in our generations are building on in various fields. Their life and works are still being valued till today. History will never forget them for their good works and selfless service to humanity.

1) GAIUS JULIUS CAESAR

He was one of the leaders in history that can't be forgotten. He was a Roman general who became leader of the government and did many things among them is the calendar we are using today. That is why it's called Julian calendar.

2) ALEXANDER THE GREAT

He was one of the ancient Greek leader who came to power after the death of his father at 20years and went on military campaign to take over territories. He had the largest empire in ancient history, he ruled the then known world from Greek to India. He achieved great work within eleven years and he died in battle before clocking 33years. He had men who served with his father who believed in his course. His success was tied with men who believed in his vision and passion. His core belief was "The brotherhood of man under the fatherhood of God" His style of leadership is being used by military leaders company owners today. He had powerful like-minded people with team-work spirit

3) SOCRATES, PLATO AND ARISTOTLE

These three men set the pace for western education and philosophy. Socrates was a Greek philosopher who founded a school and had students was helped by two of his students Plato and Aristotle. Plato help his master Socrates in his school and went to found an Academy in Athens. Aristotle remain a teacher with Plato. These men wrote books on science, philosophy, logic, poetry biology, mathematic, music government etc. There ideas are foundation on which western education is built. You can't go through university without hearing their names.

4) WILLIAM SHAKESPEARE

He was an English prolific writer and poet. His books and poems are used in literary disciplines. He is considered as one of the greatest writers in English language. His insight and imagination about life is so deep and serve as inspiration to all writers.

5) CHARLES DARWIN

He is an English geologist who came up with the theory of evolution which is generally accepted and taught in all schools worldwide.

6) GALILEO GALILEE

Galileo was an Italian mathematician, physicist, engineer, astronomer and philosopher. He invented thermos cope and various military telescope.

7) KARL HEINRICH MARX

He was a German philosopher, economics, sociologist, journalist, Politics and socialist whose work and ideas has helped in economics. He wrote book. He wrote many books with several ideas.

8) ISAAC NEWTON

Isaac was an English mathematician, physicist, astronomy, theologian whose name is known by all science with his law in physic called Newton's law of motion, law of universal gravitation. He repeated a class several times and was sent out of school.

9) ALBERT EINSTEIN

Albert was a German physicist whose work includes; theory of relativity and quantum mechanics, gravitational wave and his mass-energy equivalence formula etc. His work in the field of physics is a great challenge to the world.

10) THOMAS EDISON

Thomas Edison was an American inventor has over one thousand inventions. Every house is enjoying one of his work light. He failed many times but never gave up until he got it right. A great inventor.

These men and many others have helped to turned the world around and gave it a new name technology era. I just brought these ten for you to see. Most of them were not born with silver spoon. They had humble birth like you, but determined to make a change in their field and contribute to the world. The revolution the world has witness within the last two centuries, is more than what the world witness between creation and nineteenth centuries.

The German Wright brothers determined to do the unimaginable by setting out to make the first ever airplane. People laughed at them but they never gave in to the mockery of men. They went on with their vision until they achieved their goal they never looked back. Those who mocked them end up joining to cheer them up when they successfully launched the first ever airplane. Their value increase significantly after their presentation.

The fields of; medicine, computer, information and technology, engineering, literature, journalism, teaching and other fields has witnessed great transformations by the various contributions from men and women who chose and determine to turn the field around for good.

Bill Gate stood out in the field of computer as one of the people who has turn things around in that field and year in year out he keeps making himself relevant in such a way that you must demand for his product. Mark Zuckerberg came up with the idea of Facebook after his graduation from school. He never intended it for the world but for his school friends to keep in touch with themselves. The whole world has come to embrace this idea. The value of this man and his seven friends has since changed and the net worth has grown astronomically. There is no home in the world where their product is not being used.

Beloved, if you critically examine the lives of these valuable men who have help changed the face of the world over the centuries, you will discover that the ingredients I discussed in chapter two of this book were at play in their lives.

They are men filled with wisdom, knowledge, understanding, focus and concentrates on their goal, patience never give in to worry or anxiety, possess great ability to reason, determination, have creative ability and courageous. They are ready to risk their lives in other to achieve their vision or dream. Men of innovative, diligent in their various work. I called them dangerous men of vision with a lion heart, strength and high fliers like eagle.

If none of these things are in you, just seek ways to work on yourself to stir up these grace and once that is done, you're on your way to greatness. Your life will become the salt the whole world is looking for to sweeten their lives.

These men were indeed the salt of the earth. They all brought sweetness to the world and made it a worthy place to live for everyone. Generations to come will live to celebrate them for their good work and their names can never be forgotten on the face of the earth. Some are long dead but their works and ideas still makes them a living soul. The world is waiting for you to manifest.

CHAPTER SIX

VALUE KILLERS

"Never put off till tomorrow what may be done day after tomorrow just as well"

    Mark Twain

"If your actions inspire others to dream more, learn more, do more and become more you are a leader"

    John Kennedy

"Good moral values are mostly molded from a place where love, faith, and hope exist"

    Asenio .V. Manalo jr

When your values are clear to you, making decisions becomes easier:"

    Roy E. Disney

VALUE KILLERS

Life is a passage for everyone, many people come and go without been noticed while others cannot be forgotten. There is a common saying in my ethno group that the world is a market place. Yes indeed the world is a market place. We all come there to buy or sell. When looked critically into market setting there are also this third group called the on lookers. They didn't come to buy nor sell but just came to see what is happening in the market. Among them are those that came for window shopping. So are you a seller or buyer? If a seller what are you selling, if a buyer what are you buying? You must fall to one side. The above illustrations are correct about the world. Did God send some as seller? Sent some as buyers? And some as on lookers or spectators? My answer to these questions is; No. God sent all to come here to make impact before going back to our Maker. Someone may tell you we don't have equal destiny? Saying, some are born to be great while other are born to be poor. My humble respond to these statements is we all have equal destiny in God. The problem we have are the value or destiny killer that I will discuss in this chapter.

Do you know that everyone born into this world is a winner? There is no one born as a looser. Why? Biologist says over a million eggs are released into a woman during ejaculation. All these eggs are human beings and begin the race to meet one or two egg produced by the woman. They called this, **RACE OF LIFE**. Some dies along the way, some are washed away while others head straight into the uterus and to the fallopian tube. Only one gets to the egg and others who couldn't hit the egg are losers. That one fused with the egg to form embryo which eventually becomes every human being. The first shout or cry of baby at birth is a shout of victory that I finally make it to this side. If you are winner after the fight in the womb, how come you suddenly become a loser when you got to this world? Where is the winning spirit? How come a winner suddenly become loser? That is question to for everyone. There is no one who didn't went through this experience. Whether you are born by a king, president, the richest man or the poorest man. We all went through the same process and principle of conception and birth. Your background has nothing to do with this process. The reason why some end up a loser is what I will be discussing in this chapter. You will be able to answer those questions I asked above by the end of this chapter, once can discover your own why, you must correct yourself and advance to increase your value.

1) LIVING WITHOUT VISION OR DREAM

The percentages of the people in the world that have dream and vision for their lives are very small. Many of us come to the world expecting money and greatness to drop into our hand like the rain. Vision is an idea, goal towards which one aspires. An insight of the future of your life, career or your business. Those who have dreams or visions rules the world and can never be forgotten in history. Your vision / dream will make you be on your toes working day and night to increase your value and to become a relevant personality in the society. Money, glory and honor go in the direction of a visionary person. Men of vision are those with products sells in the market of the world. They can't be a buyer who has no product to sell. Why? They are buying products that will aid them to produce their product. They are never an on looker or spectator. They are living for their vision or their product. How big your dream will determine how well you will control the market.

If you are a man or woman without vision or dream, you will end up a spectator or on looker. Life will be frustrating for you because you have nothing you are living for. A man of vision can never be frustrated. It's your product that makes you valuable or relevant in the market. Ask yourself these questions; what is my vision for today, this week, this month or this year? What is my vision for the next five or ten years? How do I want to end my life? If there is no tangible answer, then you can't be a valued person. You can get my books **"Securing Vision"** and **"Stop Wasting Time Invest Time".** They are good materials to help wake the giant in you. It has activities to help you create a vision for yourself. Then you have what you're living for.

2) PROCRASTINATION

This is the situation where you postpone, delay, or put aside what you intend to do now till sometimes later. Procrastination is a value or vision killer the Devil is using to steal destines away. Have you noticed whatever you left undone, you end up not doing them. Any castrated animal can never produce anymore. Its glory is gone because the reproductive organ or power in him has been taken away. This is what procrastination does to anyone who allows himself or herself to be control by it. It's a big value killer. That senior friend I share his case earlier will answer me and others who disturbs him to go and finish the program: "I will go and finish the program next year". When the year comes there will be another excuse. He ends up not doing it and he never defer his admission. He lost the admission and starting all over become another problem. Distractions will not allow you to study, add new skill or improve yourself. If you do nothing about it, you will end up an on looker in this world. Don't wait for peoples' opinion as soon as you have inspiration to do something. Stop postponing events or daily activities, response immediately. Delaying is the beginning of procrastination.

3) WRONG COMPANY

"He who walks with wise men will be wise, But the companion of fools will be destroyed."

Prov 13:20 NKJV

:He who walks with the wise grows wise, but a companion of fools suffers harm."

Prov 13:20 NIV

"Become wise by walking with the wise; hang out with fools and watch your life fall to pieces."

Prov 13:20MSG

Who are your friends? Show me your friends and I will tell who you are. Wrong friends or associates will ruin your life. As you become companion with them, the message Bible said you will watch your life fall into pieces. What a great tragedy will it be. One of the major things that kills vision, dream or value are the wrong friends around you. Wrong company will make you see the wrong side of life. How bad your uncles are? How bad the government is? They make you see the various limitations around you instead of your strength. If you want to take a positive step, they are there to discouraged you that such ideas can't work with the kind of government in the world today. They can make you drop your dream for something else.

If your friends are negative people, they make you have low self-esteem. Low self-esteem is to have head down and can't look into people's eyes. You also see yourself lower than other people and give birth to photocopy of others as mentioned earlier in this book. They make you believe that some are not born great. That your background is your problem or those who supposed to help have not help. Once you give in to all their suggestions, your life and vision, dream and value will go into the air and fades away like smoke. There won't be any trace of it any more. So run away from all wrong friends or associates around you as soon as you discover.

4) SELFISHNESS

Selfishness is thinking about yourself alone all the time. Others are never important. This trait in anyone will reduce your value. Selfishness is the reason why many people steal or kill on their way up the ladder of success. The Bible says words like; "love others as yourself". "good name is better than money", "money gotten by vanity will diminish". Anyone that become rich or great through selfish means ends up losing it again. Such money or glory will soon take wings and fly away Pro23:5. We are on earth to better humanity and not to exploit them for our selfish end.

5) PRIDE

The Bible made it clear that God is against a proud person. Once you are full of pride, your value or relevancy is gone. Whatever you see as glory today will soon disappear. That is why you discover that some of those people who were rich yesterday are no more and you ask yourself, why? The reason could be that they were full of pride and God brought them down to where others like them has ended up. Satan is a good example of how pride can destroy someone. He was brought down from that great hieght God gave him to hell. Pride will make you become enemy of your Maker. There is nothing you have today that is not given to you by God. He can colloect it whenever you allow pride and you feel is by your strength you acquire them.

Always remember the rich man's story told by Jesus in Lk12:16-20. He only said in his thought, my soul rest and eat the fruit of your labor". And God answered Him tonight your soul shall be taken from you , then whose shall those things be? The man died that night and he never eat any of those things he harvested. God sees that statement as pride because he fail to acknowledge God first before he said rest my soul. He hate proud mind. Be warn. Always acknowledge Him first.

"When pride comes, then comes shame; But with the humble is wisdom."   '
Prov 11:2NKJV

"Pride goes before destruction, And a haughty spirit before a fall."

Prov 16:18 NKJV

"A man's pride will bring him low, But the humble in spirit will retain honor."

Prov 29:23 NKJV

"Wherefore he saith, God resisteth the proud, but giveth grace unto the humble."

James 4:6 KJV

6) LIVING ON PASS GLORY

Many people are found of talking about what they achieved last years of their life. They will never talk about tomorrow and what new thing they wish to achieve. Living on pass glory will make you lose your relevancy. If you celebrate your pass achievements and you are not coming to the world market with new products, no one will have anything to do with you. Going to the market with old product makes you irrelevant. Such people become frustrated of life and they are out of market. They will either become a buyer, on looker or spectator. Their value is totally gone for good. Dwelling on your past glory will prevent you from seeing the future, it could cripple your glory and make you valueless.

7) LACK OF KNOWLEDGE OR STAGNATION

This life is dynamic and not static. Likewise, knowledge is not static it's dynamic. If you have a business center filled will old IBM typewriters and computer with window 2003. You wake up one morning to open your office and close without patronage. This is because knowledge has gone beyond that level. That you're a BSc or BA holders is not important again because many people are with MSC, MA or PhD. So you remain at that level with no additional value means stagnation. Stagnation is a big time value killer. When you sit at a point doing nothing about improving yourself either to get new certificates or new skills, your value will soon disappear. New acquired knowledge makes you relevant to the society.

Beloved, value killers are what the Devil the accuser of brethren uses to make people become a no person in the society. He makes them believe that God never meant them to be great in life so he take what belongs to them. Remember he is still the Prince of this world. He seek way to control people and their wealth. Don't allow him to take over your glory and value anymore. God has put in you the seed of greatness. You are born to be great so stir up the greatness in you and don't allow any of these value killers into your life.

CHAPTER SEVEN

THE FISH WITH GOLDEN COIN

"The silver is mine gold is mine declares the almighty"
Hag 2:8 NKJV

"Every good gift and every perfect gift is from above, coming down from the Father of lights, with whom can be no variation, nor turning shadow."

James 1:17 WEB

"... For riches certainly make themselves wings; They fly away like an eagle toward heaven.
Prov 23:5 NKJV

"And God is able to provide you with every blessing in abundance,
so that you may always have enough of everything and
may provide in abundance for every good work."

2 Cor 9:8 RSV

"The Lord will make us prosperous, and our land(work) will produce rich harvests."

Ps 85:12 GNT

THE FISH WITH GOLDEN COIN

There is always a fish with the golden coin in its mouth for everyone to catch that will bring turnaround in their work, business and ministry. That is a connection that will bring end to all forms of labouring and miseries and bring them to the land of their presperity. Someone will just discover your abilities or what your company can offer thereby linking you with a source that will keep bringing business without stress. Everyone needed this kind of connection.

Jesus Christ had a situation in Mtt17:24-27 where the city tax collectors came to demand for his tax money and the accountant Mr Judas says there is no money. Possibly he had temper with the money because it's his nature to do that secretly.

"Not that he care for the poor-but he is thief, and since he was in charge of the disciples' money, he often stole some for himself."
John12:6NLT

It took a miracle for esus to be rescue from this embarrassing situation. May preachers refer to this passage on the way he was saved from embarrassement while others refer to it that we should pay all our taxes because Jesus Christ paid tax when on earth. Good as these point may be but there is a pricinple of waelth transfer we can learn from this story. Let's look carefully into the intruction Jesus gave to Peter.

" Jesus siad to them, 'Then the sonsare free. Nevertheless less we offend them, go the sea, cast in a hook, and take the fish that comes up first. And when you have opend its mouth, you will find a piece of money; take that and give it to them for Me and you."
Mtt17:26-27

Peter follow the instruction given by his Master, he got the money they needed and he paid their tax money. The following are the lessons we can learn from this drama which we can apply to our our business and we will be able to catch our own fish with the golden coin. No matter your proffession it's applicable.

1) GOD IS THE SOURCE OF ALL MONEY.

Money is spiritual and it comes from God. This bitter truth and reality of life that many find so had to understand, believe and accept. Wether you believe it or not it's the truth. Failing to believe this will make money go farther away from you. Here is what God says;

" The silver is mine, gold is mine says the Almighty"
Hag2:8
"Every good gift and every perfect gift is from above, coming down from the Father of light. With whom there can be no variations, nor turning shadows."
Jam1:17WEB
"....For money certainly make themselves wings; They fly like an eagle towards heaven"

Pro23:5bNKJV

The first and the second passages above made it clear that money or wealth comes from God. The third verse told us where it goes, heaven. Wow! Money has wings with which it could fly. That is wonderful.

God is the one who gives knowledge, wisdom, understanding, ispiration, innovations and ideas on how best you can get money. As we can see in the above story. Satan, govenment and man are not the source of money as many erroneously believed. Some may quickly says but monies are printed by the central banks. Yes they do. God sets a system in other to manage money. This is a central control for its management. If it's in the hand of individuals, they will huid it from others.

So we must come to accept this fact that God is the source of all money and we focus all our energy on the source not the wrong side. Looking somewhere else which in not the source. This will prevent you from getting what belong to you. Then we keep missing out of the blessings of God and poverty, suffering and miseries will continue. God is the true source of wealth, riches and money. Cultivate the habit of looking towards Him all the time and He will give you instructions on how you can catch your own fish with the golden coin. He will also instruct money to fly towards you, bacuse money is not needed in heaven but here on earth.

2) NEVER CUT CORNERS.

If Jesus the second person in trinity pay tax while on earth, why do his children cut corners? Never cut corners. Pay all government duties require of you and of your organization. Cutting corners is to deny yourself of true riches. This shows that your business or organization is a legitimate one and has the right to those monies printed by your country's Central Bank. Remember, the leaders are also representatives of God. That was why he requested we pray for them and wish them well. They need those taxes to meet societal needs. Refusing to pay tax is to reduce the money going to them to carry out major works and we indirectly cut or deny ourselves. Since money is spiritual.

"I urge, then, first of all, that requests, prayers, intercession and thanksgiving be made for everyone— for kings and all those in authority, that we may live peaceful and quiet lives in all godliness and holiness. This is good, and pleases God our Savior, "

1 Tim 2:1-3 NIV

"Remind your people to submit to rulers and authorities, to obey them, and to be ready to do good in every way."

Titus 3:1 GNT

Submit to the leaders as Jesus did and Devil the accuser of brethren will have no occasion against you. Pay all taxes and duties regularly.

3) MONEY FLOW IN THE DIRECTION OF YOUR SKILL.

Jesus never asked Peter to go to his former carpentry shop to sell wood. He sent him to the sea to catch fish which is the skill of Peter. The fish with golden coin is in your skill. What you're good. Peter enjoy fishing and also a professional indeed in that business. To attract money, you must enjoy your work and be professional at it. Money can never flow in your direction if you hate or complain about your work, office, business or ministry. Companies employs professional and pay them well to keep them not a novice. Do you handover your house project to a novice building engineer? No. If you do, be ready to see cracks few days after you packed in. Contract are always awarded to professional companies not the inexperience ones'. Companies will also go for the most qualified staff. Be the best in your skill and you watch your value and net worth grow significantly.

4) MONEY FOLLOWS THE SOOTHING AROMA OF LOVE AND JOY.

The one who give money, riches and wealth is love (God). You must love the source of money (God) and enjoy your skill. Be happy doing whatever you are doing now. Never complain or give any negative attitude at your work. Be joyful and be grateful to God for giving you the ability to work and to do something tangible with your hand. Money is never evil but the love for it. Most people love money more than God or their lives and other people with them. Such people has replaced God with money and he will never release it in their direction. They will only be chasing it and money will forever be playing hide and seek game with them. That is why they jump from one business to another. Jack of all trade and master of none. Money will only be available after their death to put them in the grave. Such people die laboring without result. Love God and enjoy doing your work. Peter enjoys fishing. He said this after the death of master to show that he takes pleasure in it.

"Simon Peter said to them, "I am going fishing."   *John 21:3 NKJV*

5) MONEY FLOW ACCORDING TO SPIRITUAL LAW.

Money flow according to spiritual laws established by God. Spiritual laws such; law of sowing and reaping, law of tithing, law of sacrifice, law of giving, law of first fruit etc. God has established that money, riches and wealth should respond to these laws and any other laws of this kind that has its root in God. Any other ways money comes are evil. For one to attract money you must obey one or all of these laws. That was why Jesus said Peter should go by the law of sowing and reaping. He went and did the work (sowing) of a fisherman and he caught fish (reap).

6) OBEDIENT TO INSTRUCTION AND EVERY PROMPT

Peter obeyed immediately as the instruction was given to him. You must be ready to act quickly as soon as an idea drops in your mind. Once any instruction or idea comes to you, ability and grace have been given to you to do that work. Delay might be dangerous. The fish with the coin has been released to go and wait for you as you obey. If you delay, someone else might catch the fish. As you receive an idea, so another person is also receiving the same idea. Whosoever that act first will catch the fish with the golden coin and such people's value must change.

7) GET THE RIGHT TOOLS AND MATERIALS.

To attract money in your field or skill, you must have the right tools to work effectively. The hook in Peters' hand must be sharp and not blunt. Working with bad apparatus is for you to waste time and loss customers. Be sure that all your equipment is in good other and there is backup when anyone fails. This will make you deliver your work on time and more work will keep coming. An engineer who deliver his work behind time because of weak tools, will soon be out of business while those who delivers on time because of effective tools, will soon become a ruler of that field. That is more money all the way.

8) GET THE RIGHT BAIT TO ATTRACT THE FISH.

Peter must have gotten a very good bait to attract the fish. If you're to attract the fish with the golden coin in your field get a good bait. Regular incentives, promotions are baits to attract customer. Look within your field and be inspired to put the right bait that can attract more people to patronize you. Your packaging might be a bait. Every profession has their baits, get the best to attract the right and quality fish with the golden coin. If a sheep discovers a field with enough grasses, it will surely come with other sheep when coming the second day. Remember,

"For wherever the carcass is, there the eagles will be gathered together."

Matt 24:28 NKJV

One good customer you attract and satisfy will bring many others like them. So seek ways to keep attracting more customer. Henry Ford once said "it's the customer that pays the staff not the management, so let keep satisfying them."

9) DILIGENCE

Diligence is skillfulness and hard work in your field. Peter must have been a skillful fisherman. Money flows towards diligent workers. The diligent worker will sit with kings and noble men not ordinary men. Pro22: 29. Hard work here is not hard labor. Hard work goes with wisdom while hard labor is with energy. A computer analysist who has no back up computers in his office is a hard laborer. When his system crashes or virus enter his file he will surely loss all worker. A doctor who makes his hospital look dirty, his nurse's dresses anyhow and addresses patient roughly, is an hard laborer. He may not see anybody to attend to soon. Be skillful at your work all the time. Soon your skill will attract the fish with the golden coin.

10) PATIENCE AND STEADY

In fishing, patience is highly required for you to catch a fish when you throw your line. Likewise, all profession requires a level of patience before the right customer comes. No one plant corn and expect it to grow within 24hours and after few weeks you want to harvest it. It doesn't work that way. Only children will think that way. The unfortunate thing is that most of us are like that. We start business and we are in hurry to start harvesting. There is a process time God has put in place between sowing and reaping. It can't be jump. Be patient and be steady at that work and soon the money will start flowing rapidly.

11) CONCENTRATE ON YOUR ASSIGNMENT

Concentration is focusing on your work without any distraction. We must concentrate on any task given to us. Peter can't throw his line and start looking at somewhere else. Many people are jack of all trade and end up master of none. They want to do all business in the world. As soon as someone tells them that this is the trending business, they join. They will soon move to another one because they are never patient. They are move by what people say or do. Peter concentrated until he got the fish. Concentrate on your assignment and give it your best.

12) FOCUS ON YOUR ASSIGNMENT

Focus is a process of putting all energy on ones' assignment. Let me explain; when you take a convex lens which is convergence lens under a sun and you put a paper under it, soon the paper will be burnt because the lens will converge all the sun energy on the paper. Peter also left with one focus, to get the right fish. When you focus all your energy on your assignment this way, that business must blossom and the result will bite your imagination. If you wish to diversify, be sure you've achieved success or your goal on one line of business before shifting to another one. Soon you will have chains of businesses and the flow of wealth might be uncontrollable for you. Abandoning unfinished work for another one is a calculated attempt to fail and your few resources are reducing. This will lead to emptiness and lack. Many have lost so many money this way. Be focus.

13) RIGHTLY POSITION

Moon has no light of its own but receives energy from the sun and transmit it to the earth. If it's not rightly position, there is no shinning. Peter must have try to locate a good position in that sea where he could get the good fish not anyhow fish. Jesus sent him to the sea not a river. If he had gone to a river that must have been an error. A striker on the field of football who choose to be a defend during matches will never score a goal. Ortega of Zara fashion will never locate his business in a hidden place. He locates it, on the busiest district of the city for everyone to see and today he is one of the wealthiest people in the world. Good location makes you catch the big fish with the coin. Your life, business and ministry must be rightly position to catch good customer. Locate your business in that place where your services are needed or ministry where you can impact lives. Right positioning makes the money, riches and wealth to flow in your direction and your value will surely increase.

Getting the fish with the golden coin is what every worker, business, ministry owners are daily looking for. Some are so desperate that they can do anything in the process. They believe it will come by their own power and will outside God. They end up failing in all their ways. God has established it that this fish must come to you when you approach it the right way. That was why Peter succeeded in that mission and the money was enough to settle their taxes and they were never embarrassed. Peter went on a mission to obey his master and to get the fish. There is nothing that could distract a man on a mission, they are focused, determined and diligent in their work or business. That is the secret to wealth and riches and you must succeed.

Settle down and take a good look at your own business or ministry to see where you have gone off the track and you have been chasing the shadow of money, riches or wealth. Shadow is never the same with the real thing. God didn't design us to chase money but money is meant to flow or fly in our direction as we obey all his laws. God said;

"Blessed shall you be in the city, and blessed shall you be in the country. Blessed shall be the fruit of your body, the produce of your ground and the increase of your herds, the increase of your cattle and the offspring of your flocks."

Deut 28:3-4NKJV

This is blessing following you and not the reverse. If reverse its laboring and not blessing. God is very straight in this passage and he own the earth and the fullness thereof.

"The earth is the Lord's, and everything in it, the world, and all who live in it; (Man, woman, animals, Birds, Fishes and all solid and liquid minerals including the currencies.)

Ps24:1NIV

He told Nebuchadnezzar that he gives the kingdom of the earth to whosoever he will. Satan or any other person were not there when he was busy making all we can see physically on the earth today. So we all must come to that level of right positioning like this for our value and net worth to increase. As you reposition yourself, business or ministry in the right direction of God who has all it takes to change all things. If you critically examine all the major business or ministry owners around you and in the world, you will discover that it's those who are following these points brought out of the story of Peter and the fish with the coin that are really attracting money and increasing their net worth. Get on your assignment and be the Peter on a mission in that field to get the first fish with the golden coin to increase value and net worth.

CHAPTER EIGHT

THE OIL OF SERVICE

"You need an attitude of service. You're not just serving yourself. You help others to grow up and you grow with them"

David Green

"To give real service you must add something which cannot be bought or measure with money and that is sincerity and integrity"

Douglas Adams

"The thighest of distinction is service to other"

King Geaorge V1

"Your service to others that is effective, efficient and acceptable is what brings true happiness and more than enough wealth"

Oluwafemi Dennis Ojo

"Always render more and bether service than is expected of you, no matter what your task may be"

Og Mondino

"Fame, power, glory and wealth is on the wings of service you render to humanity and nature"

Oluwafemi Deniis Ojo

THE OIL OF SERVICE

Service is rendering assistance to someone or humanity. God set all elements; oxygen, nitrogen, carbon 1V oxide, sun, moon, ocean, sea, river, birds and all other animals were created to render service to the world. For as long they continue to render their service as it should be, God keep replenishing them. Ever since the air has been rendering its service of supporting nature, it hasn't finished. The service of the sun and moon has been since the beginning of the world. They haven't changed and they keep rendering their services to the Universe. The Universe have a way of paying them back and to renew them so that their service can continue. This system will continue till the end of the world.

The coming of Jesus to the world was to render service to the world and to God. The Bible says he went about doing good to people by healing the sick, raising the dead and redeem man from the power of sin and to reconcile them to God. He wasn't going from place to places because he target the money or gift he will receive from people. It was rendering a selfless service to humanity and God. He sees himself as a gift to the world. Do you know that you're also a gift to the world like Jesus? The compensation that came at the end of his work on earth, is far greater than what human mind could imagine. The value and the power that follows is also greater than what demons or anyone could comprehend. God made his name greater than all names in heaven on earth and in the world beneath.

"And being found in fashion as a man, he humbled himself, and became obedient unto death, even the death of the cross. Wherefore God also hath highly exalted him, and given him a name which is above every name: That at the name of Jesus every knee should bow, of things in heaven, and things in earth, and things under the earth; and that every tongue should confess that Jesus Christ is Lord, to the glory of God the Father."

Phil 2:8-11 KJV

Jesus first render effective, efficient service without complaining he faced the most disgraceful and painful death and God blessed and honor him. This should be the bases for all our service. Once this is so you're bound to get high reward at the end of the service.

Peter was approached by Jesus in Luke chapter five for the service of his boat and he got a high compensation at the end of the service. Peter had just come back from a hard night of laboring without result and was about to go home empty when Jesus approached him. He had the chance of turning down the request because of the ugly experience he and his associate had. He gladly rendered the service and had a great reward at the end of the service greater than what he would have caught overnight with all his expertise at work.

"When he had finished speaking, he said to Simon, "Put out into the deep, and let down your nets for a catch." Simon answered him, "Master, we worked all night, and took nothing; but at your word I will let down the net." When they had done this, they caught a great multitude of fish, and their net was breaking. They beckoned to their partners in the other boat, that they should come and help them. They came, and filled both boats, so that they began to sink. But Simon Peter, when he saw it, fell down at Jesus' knees, saying, "Depart from me, for I am a sinful man, Lord." For he was amazed, and all who were with him, at the catch of fish which they had caught;

Luke 5:4-9 WEB

The reward of his service was so great that his associates and other fishermen around him got blessed. That is what comes when service is rendered the right way. True service will change your value and also increase your net-worth so much that people around you will be blessed through it.

Every work and services we render are to be like the service of Peter that was not for any gain but to meet the need of someone who is in dear need. They are to be seen as good service that makes life and the world worth living for everyone. The product of your company should be produce to add value and color to the world and not for selfish gain. Once they are established on this platform of service, it will grow and last for many years to come and the gain that will follows will bit your imagination. The following are the points to draw from the service of Peter to Jesus Christ. They will help bring change of value and also increase your net worth.

1) SERVICE SHOULD BE EFFECTIVE AND EFFICIET

Peter rendered willing service without complaining and it was effective and efficient one indeed. He never allowed his emotion to affect his decision or dictate for him. In rendering our service, we are to target effectiveness and efficiency so that people can keep demanding our service. Any service rendered with complaining and grumbling, will end up not attract reward. Because it won't be rendered effectively and efficiently. For as long as your service is effective and efficient it will attract more patronage and it's this that will bring the wealth you strongly desire. What people look for in service is effectiveness and efficiency.

2) SOLVE A MAJOR PROBLEM

Peter solve a major problem of Jesus Christ that day. He was looking for a platform to reach out to people and he made his boat available. Your service must solve a major company or societal problem. If the reason you go to that office is to make money, you will never see yourself contributing to the growth of the office. You may not go far because you will not see any reason why you need to increase your skill and knowledge. Once you see yourself as someone to solve a problem like Jesus and Peter in that office you will soon become a manager. Your company product should solve a major problem of people. Facebook, WhatsApp and other social applications solve major problem in the society. Telephone make communication easier. The more effective and efficient the telecom service is to people the more patronage and more money in the wallet of the owners. Amazon, Alibaba, eBay and other ecommerce and emarket organizations around the world make marketing and buying easy for people every day This service has changed the value and increase net worth of the owners.

Many authors that would have end up within their country has known worldwide because self-publishing applications like kindle, Publish drive, Ejunkie, Draft to Digit, kobo, Smash work, iuniverse other similar platforms. The authors and the owner of those platforms' value and net worth has change greatly. They've made book publishing easy.

DHL, FedEx, Ems and other logistics organization are making logistics easier. This role in the society has made them to in high demand. There in nowhere in the world where their presence hasn't been felt. Bottle and sachet water has made good and potable water available to people to reduce the rate at which diarrhea or typhoid is spreading. Once the target of that company is to solve a given problem of people, the demand on that company's product will increase daily and before long it will become a worldwide organization.

3) DON'T PUT PRICE BEFORE THE SERVICE

Peter didn't render that service on the condition that he will be paid certain amount before he render the service. He rendered it freely and he was paid greatly. This doesn't mean that we shouldn't put price on our goods before we put them on sale. That shouldn't be the reason for the product rather the role it will play in the life of whosever buys it and use it. Our focus and drive shouldn't be on the money but the service rendered and the good product we are given to the people. Good service will attract more than you ever bargain for. When people sees how effcient your product is, it will become a generally accpeted one and you end up getting more money for many years to come.

4) SERVICE SHOULD BE IN YOUR EXPERTISE

Service are to be rendered in the area of your expertise. Peter knows how to handle boat so he was able to keep the boat steady for Jesus to deliver his sermon. Your service should be given out in the area where you're the best. Give your best at all time so as to change your value.

5) ONCE BLESSED, BLESS OTHERS

Peter got blessed after the service he rendered. The blessing was so much that he blessed other people around him. He had the room to keep it to himself but he became a blessing to others. Wealth goes in circle, once the circle is broken, it will stop flowing. To keep it flowing bless the challenged people around you. You need the prayer of this people. This is the reason some engages in philanthropist and humanitarian. Their prayer goes a long way to turn things around in your life.

CHAPTER NINE

CAPACITY BUILDING

"Capacity building requires a deliberate effort or energy to learn, absorb information with pains, rigor that you are not ready to forgo"

Oluwafemi Dennis Ojo

"Growing your leadership capacity demands personal effectiveness. Being effective is the ability to do the right thing all the times no matter the cost"

Ifeanyi Enoch Onuoha

"To succeed in life, you must build the capacity to go through failure and the resistance from allowing the failure go through you"

Awolumate Samuel

"Capacity building is the ability to let go of today's pleasure with your life on the line to grow and develop for you to rule tomorrow"

Oluwafemi Dennis Ojo

"The more people I am able to help the more people are willing to help others. The more followers we have, the closer we are to a perfect world"

Akiinathan Logeswaran

"The quantity and quality of your content is your capacity and that is what makes you relevant to the world."

Oluwafemi Dennis Ojo

CAPACITY BUILDING

Capacity has many definitions depending on the side you look at it. Capacity is the ability to hold, receive and absorb substance. Capacity is also the ability to perform a given task or assignment. Capacity is the ability or the power to learn or acquire knowledge. Capacity is the ability in anyone to carry out a specific function or task. Capacity is the potential in anything to grow and develop.

All of these definitions are relevant to our subject of increasing your value or net worth. The capacity in anyone is the ability to learn, absorb, perform any function or task given without complain and develop in your character, abilities, potentials, business or ministry. Once you're not ready to build capacity, your value will never change and your net worth will remain the same. That is the reason why great people never joke with capacity building because they know that is what will announce them to the world.

Men of high capacity are like military mines buried in the soil waiting for someone to step on it. The area with mines doesn't look different on the surface but has something buried inside it. It's the buried substances that makes it different. As soon as you step on the mines, that is when you will know the capacity of what has been buried within that area. Pam! It will explode and everything changes. The men with capacity only need one avenue to express themselves, and what they have labor to build over time will explode and people around them will be surprise at what such men has been carrying. Capacity building is a must for anyone who want to control or rule any field in the world. It's what you have that people are waiting for. The quantity and quality of your content is your capacity and that is what makes you relevant to the world. That is what will open door for them to celebrate you. If you have nothing to offer you're not better than them anyone else, there is nothing to celebrate in you. People are looking for men who are better than them. Seek to know what other people don't know or do what others can't do and they will give you a standing ovation at your appearance.

Let's link capacity building to the Bible so we can learn how we can build capacity and change the way people see us. When you focus on building capacity, and you never compromise your stand, few months down the line could cause a significant changes in your life. Let's look at few people and analysis how they build capacity and what happen after.

MOSES

Moses was born by a Hebrew woman at a time when Pharaoh was having a good time and enjoying the servanthood of the Israelite. He happens to be train and brought up in the palace of the man who is killing the Jews. Isn't God great? He realized that he is a Hebrew and begins to scheme on how to deliver his people without much capacity, but failed. He ran away to the land of Midian and remain there for forty years where he learnt how to control himself and lead through the animal of his father-in-law. He also develops a solid relationship with God. He was the only man who speaks mouth to mouth with God in the Bible. That investment of forty years' changes things in his life and when he returned, he become a leader to all Israel and god to Pharaoh. His brother Aaron became his prophet. Isn't that wonderful? He later wrote laws as a guide to the children of Israel on how to follow God. He wrote five books of the scripture and many Psalms and songs. The result of capacity building. The Bible says;

"By faith Moses, when he became of age, refused to be called the son of Pharaoh's daughter, choosing rather to suffer affliction with the people of God than to enjoy the passing pleasures of sin,"

Heb 11:24-25NKJV

Capacity building requires a deliberate effort or energy to learn, absorb information with pains, rigor that you are not ready to forgo. Who could have imagined that Moses will prefer to be slave than to be refer to as crown prince? He ran away to become a servant to his father-in-law. That is what capacity building requires. If you're not ready to forgo today's enjoyment, you can't grow, build or develop capacity and your value will ever remain the same.

JEPHTHAH

"Now Jephthah of Gilead was a great warrior. He was the son of Gilead, but his mother was a prostitute. Gilead's wife also had several sons, and when these half-brothers grew up, they chased Jephthah off the land. "You will not get any of our father's in-

heritance," they said, "for you are the son of a prostitute." So Jephthah fled from his brothers and lived in the land of Tob. Soon he had a band of worthless rebels following him."

Judg 11:1-3 NLT

Jephthah was one of the sons of Gilead but was born by an illegal wife. Naturally this man was supposed not to be one of the sons to reckon with among the sons of his father. Other children show this by rejecting him and making him realize that he is a no person. Someone without value and can't become prominent in the family and in their society. This rejection made him to leave his fathers' house to another location. While these legal children are busy enjoying the pleasure of the house, he was busy building capacity in physical fitness and handling weapon of war. This made the worthless men who may have been rejected like to gathered around him and all became men of war who could handle weapon of war. Their value and potentials increase significantly and their company became a major group they use for security and defense. A time will always come when your gifts, skills, potentials will make way for you or announce you to the world. A came when the children of Ammon made war against Israel. It was so, that when the children of Ammon made war against Israel, the elders of Gilead went to get Jephthah out of the land of Tob, and they said to Jephthah, Come and be our chief, that we may fight with the children of Ammon.

A no person became the leader of Israel not his father's house where he was rejected. His value changed and increased more than his brothers who had earlier rejected him. But because he devoted time in building capacity and also worked on himself, his value changed greatly.

DAVID

He stood out tall among the whole Israel because he took time to build capacity. The Bible didn't mention why he was sent to be with the flocks of his father at that tender age. But why he was there, he was diligent in keeping those flocks without complains. He was ready to defend them from all wild animals. He builds enough capacity why in the wilderness. The capacity he builds was what enable him to kill Goliath. Here is what he said to the king before facing Goliath.

"But David said to Saul, "Your servant has been keeping his father's sheep. When a lion or a bear came and carried off a sheep from the flock, 35 I went after it, struck it and rescued the sheep from its mouth. When it turned on me, I seized it by its hair, struck it and killed it."
1 Sam 17:34-35 NIV

Capacity building is the ability to let go of today's pleasure with your life on the line to grow and develop for you to rule tomorrow. David put his life on the line at that tender age to kill lion and bear when building capacity. Other children of his age were at home under their father but he was in the wilderness building capacity. That was why they never had the same result. He left children play to learn how to take responsibility. No wonder he became a champion. The ability he had to kill Goliath was acquired in the wilderness. Goliath and lion or bear are not the same. His capacity announced him after killing Goliath. One throw of the stone, down Goliath went and David exploded. He became a champion by that killing. That capacity you've built. needs just one open door and you will be announced like David. The pains and rigors worth it once the announcement comes.

DANIEL AND HIS FRIENDS

Daniel and his friends were also men who increase their value by the capacity they built over three years in the Babylonian school.

"But Daniel resolved not to defile himself with the royal food and wine, and he asked the chief official for permission not to defile himself this way."
Dan 1:8 NIV
"God gave the four young men knowledge and skill in literature and philosophy. In addition, he gave Daniel skill in interpreting visions and dreams."
Dan 1:17GNT

"In every matter of wisdom and understanding about which the king questioned them, he found them ten times better than all the magicians and enchanters in his whole kingdom."
Dan 1:20 NIV

They were not ready to compromise themselves or their standards. This was an opportunity for them to loss control and say what a privilege and enjoy themselves as children of their age would have done. But they decided to give themselves to serious studying and eating less. When the time of examination came, they were ten times better than other students in that school. They became governors and adviser to the king. Leader, Pastors, student and teachers should learn from these young boys. Dedicate yourself to more study, it will only make you better than others and put you in position of honor like Daniel and his friends.

DISCIPLES OF JESUS

The men who were timid when Jesus Christ was alive change things in their live and ministry by building capacity. Peter denied Jesus to his face before a young girl because of fear. The whole story changed when they build capacity. They were at the upper room because of fear for many days building capacity through prayer and reading the scripture.

"They all joined together constantly in prayer, along with the women and Mary the mother of Jesus, and with his brothers."
Acts 1:14 NIV

"When the day of Pentecost came, they were all together in one place. Suddenly a sound like the blowing of a violent wind came from heaven and filled the whole house where they were sitting. They saw what seemed to be tongues of fire that separated and came to rest on each of them. All of them were filled with the

"Holy Spirit and began to speak in other tongues as the Spirit enabled them."
Acts 2:1-4 NIV

The whole fear in them changed after they were filled with the Holy Spirit. They were able to stand before the Pharisee and other leaders when the have built, and develop capacity. Their value changed and people were afraid of them. If they didn't devote time to prayer and reading of the scripture, things wouldn't have change in their live. Capacity require serious rigors and pains you chose to ignore.

JESUS CHRIST

The second person in trinity also build capacity before coming into public ministry. He never steps out and start his ministry because he is the word of God. He was in the wilderness for forty day and night praying without food, friends and family. Capacity build time is the period of self-denial of all pleasures which could serve as distractions. Satan visited him tried to tempt him as he did to Adam and changed the course of life. Jesus was a better focused man than Adam and Eve. He was man on a mission ready to give all he has for his course. Which he eventually did. After this period Jesus returned in the power of Holy Spirit and things changed in his life.

"Jesus returned to Galilee in the power of the Spirit, and news about him spread through the whole countryside."

Luke 4:14 NIV

The glory of Jesus changed and his fame spread everywhere in the country of Israel. The man was no longer the same as the carpenter they use to know. Power came onto his life ministry and his changed completely. He never went back into the carpentry shop. Because the new capacity is bigger and better than that of a carpenter. His Nazareth people has this to say.

"Is not this the carpenter's son? is not his mother called Mary? and his brethren, James, and Joses, and Simon, and Judas? And his sisters, are they not all with us? Whence then hath this man all these things?"

Matt 13:55-56 KJV

The man is no longer the same. Capacity has changed and his glory has shone for the whole world to see. People come everywhere to see him. They knew him when was still going around as carpenter. Some may still be owing him. That doesn't matter anymore. That was an old glory. His life became a mystery to everyone in his home town. This is how it will be for anyone who labor to build capacity. So pastors, preacher and teach of the cross, that time of prayer and studying is not a waste. You're building capacity. Even though it looks as if nothing is happening, continue your time of announcement is around the corner.

Increasing your value requires hard work in the place of building capacity. It's never easy but it worth it. Satan must have target the time when Jesus was weak and he seriously need food. He said, why not change this stone to bread and eat? You don't have to labor or punish yourself this way? But Jesus replied to him shows that he wasn't ready t compromise. Man is not meant to live by food all the time. This means there're time we need to deny ourselves because we are building capacity so as to increase our value and change our net worth. Your time of capacity building is never a time of time wasting, it's a time of investment that must yield bountifully harvest.

If all these people have to build capacity before they're announcement, we all need to build capacity if we must increase our value and net worth. It's what you've gather over time that becomes your new personality that the world will celebrate. None of these men remain the same. Their status change, position in the society changed, the view of people about them also changed. Can you imagine the brothers of David calling him sir and bowing for him? When your capacity changes, respect, honor, dignity and even money follows to you. People brings business to you on their own. Government reserves certain work for you in the budget. They know your company is the only one that has the capacity to do the work. Can you see that money flow to you on its own accord? You will no longer struggle for contract. Money is not an issue for you again. Focus on capacity building in your field and your value and net worth will grow astronomically.

CHAPTER TEN

THE OIL OF FRUITFULNESS

"Then God blessed them, and God said to them, "Be fruitful and multiply; fill the earth and subdue it; have dominion over the fish of the sea, over the birds of the air, and over every living thing that moves on the earth."

Gen 1:28NKJV

"Your fruitfulness begins with you understanding your place in God's program and your fruits will begin to manifest"

Oluwafemi Dennis

"you win when you are able to convert that time into an investment, into seeds or fruits or products of cultivating your own land or products in other people's lives"

Sunday Adelaja

THE OIL OF FRUITFULNESS

Fruitfulness was first used in the Bible when God was pronouncing blessing on man. It then means that as children of God, we are designed to be fruitful in whatever we do and where so ever we go according to the program of our maker. In the scriptures below, God has given man the grace to be fruitful. If you're nor fruitful is your making.

"And God blessed them, and God said unto them, Be fruitful, and multiply, and replenish   the earth, and subdue it: and have dominion over the fish of the sea, and over the fowl of the air, and over everything that move upon the earth"

Gen 1:28 KJV

"...and whatsoever he (man) doeth shall prosper"

P s1:3 KJV

This was repeated again in the Abrahamic covenant blessing.

"...and I will make of thee a great nation, and I will bless the, and make thy name great and thou shalt be a blessing:"

Gen 12:2 KJV

One person, becoming a great nation and his name also becoming a channel of blessing is fruitfulness. Fruitfulness is defined as the ability or power to produce fruits or young ones'. It also means having good result in abundance. God's mind for man is for him to replicate what he (God) can do. The power to produce is within man by the pronouncement of God into his life at creation. And by the spirit of God on us we are meant to be fruitful and multiply daily.

"And God said let us make man in our own image after our likeness........,,so God created man in in his own image in the image of God created he him, male and female created he them.

Gen 1:25-25

God want man to live and constantly have a productive life.

That's why God blessed man with the grace of fruitfulness. Anything that opposes this in our life is of the Devil and should be greatly resist at all cost. God compares the fruitfulness in man with two trees in the book of Psalm; palm and cedars.

"The righteous shall flourish like the palm tree: he shall grow like a cedar in Lebanon"

Ps92:12 KJVKJV

What kind of trees are palm trees and cedars? A palm tree is any of the evergreen plant found in the tropical regions of the world. A palm tree survives and flourish in any where it grows. Every part of it is useful; the leaves, stem, it juices and fruits are good as cooking oil and kernel oil is used for soap production. The kernel is also medicinal. Palm trees grows upright and hardly bend. No matter how severe the storm, it hardly breaks. Palm trees are emblem of victory because any changes in the weather doesn't affect their fruitfulness. They produce throughout the year. The man created is designed to be productive in all areas like a palm tree this way. A palm tree is like a tree planted by the rivers of water, it gives it fruits as at when requires.

"And he shall be like a tree planted by the river of water that brings forth his fruit in his season, his leaf also shall not wither; whatsoever he do shall prosper"

Ps1:3 NKJV

God want to see every man and woman to be fruitful in this manner. If God want to see you as he sees the palm tree, you shouldn't see yourself order wise. You're a fruitful personality on earth.

A cedar tree on the other hand is any of several old-world evergreen coniferous tree of the genus cedrus in the family Panacea having stiff needles on short shoots and large erect seed cones with broad deciduous scales. The tree is found in the Middle east, Himalayas, Alaska and Greece and grows to a height of 200feet. Cedars trees stays for many years, free of fire, resistance to pests and diseases. They are also used for healing, purification and spiritual protection. Its spiritual; properties are supposed to promote peaceful thoughts and help interpret messages from the inner self. The wood is used for the door of sacred temples and burned in cleaning ceremonies for purification. The people in the areas where cedars grows don't joke with it, they cherish it. Cedars has pleasant smell and odor. They are used for construction of boat, canoes, weapon of war, bowels, boxes, blankets, caps, writing pencils and making costumes etc.

God bless palm trees and cedars this way and makes them useful for many purposes, their fruitfulness is incomparable. God want man to be useful and fruitful in this manner. The righteous must flourish and fruitful like palm trees and cedars. The grace of fruitfulness is in you, and you must activate the grace so as to increase your value.

Then oil of fruitfulness drip on you the moment you make up your mind to follow and to do the bidding of the Lord. You must flourish in all your ways and whatsoever you lay your hands on to do. His word says and you shall prosper in whatsoever you do. Who will prosper and who will flourish? The righteous. The righteous will daily experience the flow of the oil of fruitfulness in their lives.

"You prepare a table before me in the presence of my enemies: you anointed my head with OIL, my cup runs over"

Ps23:5NKJV

God will even make you to be fruitful in the presence of your enemies. No matter how wicked or ferocious they may look, they

will watch you fruitful on every side and they can't do anything about it. Because the Lord has anointed your head with oil of fruitfulness. Hallelujah! What a wonderful oil and life God has programed for the righteous. What God said makes king David comes to mind.

"I have found David my servant, with my holy OIL have I anointed him: with whom my hand shall be establish: mine arm also shall strengthen him. The enemies shall not exact upon him; nor the son of wickedness afflict him. And I will beat down his foes before his face, and I will plague them that hate him." *Ps89:20-23KJV*

God defended, protected, established King David because of his

OIL on his head. God beat down all his enemies before him. Goliath fell upon his face to the earth before David in 1 Sam17: 49. Saul kept on failing until he finally died at Gilboa according to the prophesy of Samuel in 1Sam26:10. The oil of fruitfulness defends you from trouble and enemies and it will establish you in life. Total obedience to the laws and commandments of God keeps your head fresh with the oil of fruitfulness.

And it shall come to pass if thou shall harken diligently unto the thy God, to observed and to do all his commandment which I command thee this day, that the Lord thy God will set thee on high above all nations of the earth: and all these blessings shall come thee, and overtake thee, if thou shall harken unto the voice of the Lord thy God. Blessed shall thou be in the city, and blessed thou be in the field. Blessed shall be the fruit of thy body, and the fruit of thy ground, and the fruit of thy cattle, the increase of sheep. Blessed shall be thy basket and thy store. Blessed shall thou be when thou come in, and blessed shall thou be when thou go out. The Lord shall cause thy enemies that rise up against thee to be smitten before thy face: they shall come out against thee in one way, and flee before thee seven ways.

The Lord shall command the blessing upon thee in thy store houses and in all that thou set thy hand unto: and shall bless thee in the land which the Lord thy God giveth thee. The Lord shall establish thee and holy people unto himself as he has sworn unto thee if thou shall keep the commandment of the Lord thy God, and walk in his ways.

Deu28:1-9 KJV

The scripture above defined the full fruitfulness God has set aside for anyone who choose to follow his commandments, your value net worth can never remain the same, it must increase. Abraham and David started small when they key to obedient, their value changed and they became great in their generation and reference point to generations after them.

Abraham became rich by the wonderful steps taken by the way he aligned himself with the ordinances of God. He went to rescue his nephew Lot and his family after Sodom was invaded by a stronger king. He brought back all the captives with the spoils but Abraham give all he brought back to other people and the king of Sodom Gen14:16-24. The only thing he took was to pay the tithe of the spoils to Melchizedek who in turn declares the blessing of God on him. Can you also imagine the joy in the heart of people whom he brought back and those he blessed? Everyone will surely be declaring God's blessing on him. God will back it up because he put simile on people's faces.

When you obey the law of tithing, you open yourself for God's blessing and you must be fruitful in whatever you put your hands to do.

"Bring the whole tithe into the storehouse, that there may be food in my house. Test me in this," says the Lord Almighty, "and see if I will not throw open the floodgates of heaven and pour out so much blessing that you will not have room enough for it. I will prevent pests from devouring your crops, and the vines in your fields will not cast their fruit," says the Lord Almighty. "Then all the nations will call you blessed, for yours will be a delightful land," says the Lord Almighty."

Mal 3:10-12NIV

Obedient to the law of tithing connects you with God's oil of fruitfulness. In the above scripture, God said he will open his store house and pure out his blessings and wealth will surely flow in your direction. The world will surely be amazed with the way and manner you will be blessed. What other people are doing and they not succeeding, will just work without stress with you. This because God in with you giving you inspirations and power to progress and proper and gather wealth.

"But remember the Lord your God, for it is he who gives you the ability to produce wealth ....."

Deut 8:18 NIV

Depending on your own strength and wisdom will only amount to hardship and laboring. Get connected to God's oil of fruitfulness and life becomes easier for you. Effortless wealth and glory comes to you. That was the secret of Abraham wealth. It's still working for as long as you connect to it and do as God instructed.

David on the other hand became very wealthy after the Ziklag experience by the wonderful step he took. God told him to pursue, overtake and recover his family whom he had lost to the invaders when he wasn't around. He in deed recover them and got so much spoils from the invaders. He should have said this is the blessing of God for me and keep all to himself as most people would have done. He shared things for all his men those that went and those that couldn't go, send gifts to all the people who has ever helped him. He even sent part of the gift to Judah. This singular action connected him to God's oil of blessing. The Bible says;

"A man's gift makes room for him, And brings him before great men." Prov *18:16NKJV*

After this action by David, the people of Hebron came to him that he should come and rule over them. That gift activated the anointing kingship on him. The gift you gift out is to opens you up to more blessing and to make you seat with special people. James told the church that heling the needy is the true religion ordain by God.

"Pure and genuine religion in the sight of God the Father means caring for orphans and widows in their distress and refusing to let the world corrupt you."

James 1:27NLT

Once you've started making little by little cultivate the habit of helping people and the needy around you. Remember givers never lack. Because as they keep scattering they will be increasing. Your value and net worth will never remain the same as you make giving a habit is your life. The Bile says;

"There is one who scatters, yet increases more; And there is one who withholds more than is right, but it leads to poverty. The generous soul will be made rich, and he who waters will also be watered himself."

Prov 11:24-25 NKJV

The principle is the more you give, the more you receive, the greater you become. While the less you give. the lesser you receive. the poorer you become. The choice is yours. David shared and he became king. Helping people is helping yourself. So don't see helping the needy as a burden, but a privilege giving to you by God to put simile on the faces of people. When you give to the needy, you're giving to God. Whatsoever you do to these people you're going it for God. Said Jesus while talking to his disciples. So be happy and glad doing it, it's the true religion that pleases God. Anyone that pleases God is a special person and God must surely bless him. His blessing come in a wonderful way.

"To the man who pleases him, God gives wisdom, knowledge and happiness, but to the sinner he gives the task of gathering and storing up wealth to hand it over to the one who pleases God...."

Eccl 2:26 NIV

Can you imagine what God promised to do in the above passage? He will give the sinners power to gather treasure and wealth. He will give to the man who has pleased him wisdom or ideas through which he will collect the wealth the disobedient people had labored to gather for years. Is God wicked? No. He is only blessing his obedient children. These obedient children are so special that God can do anything for them. Because he is sure that whatever he gives them, will be share among many people. Do you see something in that passage that the sinners don't share? They only store up their wealth for themselves. This is against the principle of God. It's of the Devil? Storing up wealth is to deny others and the needy? That is the reason why God will give you special wisdom in your field to collect from them what they have labor to gather. This is how God gives his children power to get wealth. Your sharing it to the needy, and the good ideas you're coming up with is wealth creation. This is the real blessing and it goes with special oil called oil of fruitfulness. In Den 28:1-14 God listed what will happen in the life of anyone who has make his life like Abraham and David. Those who love God not because they want him to bless them or make them great. But they love him and obey all his commands because a necessity is laid on them. They see obeying God as a way of life and a task that must be done.

It flows effortlessly in them. Is whatever condition things turn around them, they are not moved and will never see God as the evil working against them. They take responsibilities for all their actions and look forward each day to God for help and a better life. That is why you see such people moving from glory to glory.

Oil of fruitfulness is the oil of success and prosperity. All the men mentioned in this book were anointed like Abraham and David. That is why you can know them. They were indeed blessed in all their works and were blessings to many generations by their works. Generations are still partaking in that blessing because they left inheritance for their children. They were indeed good seller in this world and their products are blessing and it's still selling. What a fruitful life?

"He shall be like a tree Planted by the rivers of water, that brings forth its fruit in its season, whose leaf also shall not wither; And whatever he does shall prosper."

Ps 1:3NKJV

They were like tree planted by the rivers of water flourishing all they time. This a great oil and grace from God to such people's life. Their work prospers and wealth flows in their direction uncontrollably. They are strong determinant of the world market. If they choice to pull out of market, nations will cry and lives will be affected. Can you imagine thousands that will be out of business if Amazon should close down suddenly? Many. I will affect the economy of America. Check out many other establishments like that?

God is the source of all wealth. He owns the earth and all that are in it; man, animals, birds, fishes and all treasures in it. He put man as the manager it. Those words declared on man in Genesis 1:28 hasn't be revoked. They are still effective in anyone's life who recognizes God and his words. That is why above scripture says such man will be blessed in all his works or business. God knows best you can be blessed. The scripture also says;

"Every good gift and every perfect gift is from above, and cometh down from the Father of lights, with whom is no variableness, neither shadow of turning. "

James 1:17

Will commands the blessing in your direction no one can reverse it or oppose it. He has the perfect gift, blessing, promotion, job, wife, husband, children and wealth in his room in heaven. They will only manifest whenever you're rightly connected. Looking somewhere else for your blessing is a waste of time and energy. If he says you're blessed that is enough to hold on to and focus on your work and that blessing will surely flow down from God. Just ensure that all the ingredients that increase value or worth are at work in your life or organization.

As God is a spirit and his words are spiritual so are his blessings. You must believe it first before they will start flowing down. Wealth, money, honor and Glory are also spiritual. They flow onto lives as we obey his instructions. That was what we read earlier in Deu 28:1-2. If you jump these two verses and start claiming from verse 3-14, we are only deceiving yourself. The fulfillment of the blessings is in your obedience of the first two verses.

Let me close this chapter with this scripture below possibly you will have a clear understanding of what am saying.

" But if you look closely into the PERFECT LAW that SETS PEOPLE FREE, and keep on paying attention to it and do not simply listen and then forget it, but put it into PRACTICE — you will be BLESSED by God in what you do."

James 1:25 GNT

The above scripture says you must look carefully into the laws of God. Then set your mind to practice it. This action will make whatever you put your hands on to prosper. Stop seeing the scriptures as words of ordinary man. Set your mind to obey them. This is because we all came from God and we will return to him one day to give account of our works on earth. Increasing you value outside God is to open your life, business and family for Satan to mess us up. His blessing is full of enough sorrow. But God's blessings are without sorrow. Prov22 *"The blessing of the Lord makes a person rich, and he adds no sorrow with it."*

He doesn't have free gift. Whatever Satan gives you something with the right hand, he collects it with his left hand. Plenty of troubles, sorrow, pains and sickness follows the blessing of Satan. Run away from him and embrace God who gives abundantly and takes away your troubles, sorrows, sickness and pains so you can enjoy it. Jesus said this about Satan;

"The thief comes only in order to steal and kill and destroy. I came that they may have and enjoy life, and have it in abundance (to the full, till it overflows)."

John 10:10 AMP

Satan purpose is to make you part of his companion in the eternal lake of fire at the end of your work on earth. He is a thief that comes to steals, kill your dream, and give you his own dream that will lead you into eternal destruction. Rev 21: 5

Jesus make it clear here that he came to give us all things that pertains to life and godliness and to have all things in abundance and to overflow. Overflow health, wealth and honor. Believing and accepting Jesus Christ as your Lord and Savior is all for your benefit. The last part says as you keep practicing the law, you will be blessed in whatever business, work or whatever engages you. God will bless you to overflowing. It's that wonderful? My sincere desire for everyone reading this book is to come to this understanding and change their life completely and begin to enjoy the blessings of God. Get connected to this oil of fruitfulness today, your value will change and your net worth will grow significantly and you will become one of the wealthiest giants in the world.

CHAPTER ELEVEN

THE POWER OF CHOICE

"Sometimes it's the smallest decisions that can change your life forever"

Keri Rusell

"We are the creative force of our life, and through our own decisions rather than our conditions, if we carefully learn to do certain things, we can accomplish those goals"

Stephen Covey

"Life present you with so many decisions. A lot of times, they're really difficult, but we must make them"

Brittany Mushy

THE POWER OF CHOICE

The Lord has given to us the power to choose whatever we will for ourselves and career. The power of choice has been left with man. Joshua makes this clear to all Israel before his departure. Moses also made similar statement to the same people as a revelation of the mind of God for the world.

"I call heaven and earth to record this day against you, that I have set before you; life and death, blessing and curse; therefore, choose life, that both thou and thy seed may live"

Deu30:19 KJV

"And if it seem evil unto you to serve the Lord, choose you this day whom you will serve…. But as for me and my house we will serve the Lord"

Josh24:15 KJV

"And the people said unto Joshua, the Lord our God will we serve, and his voice will we obey"

Josh24:24KJV

That you obey or disobey God, is the power of choice. Everyone that engages in evil deeds or wickedness around the world today, chooses that path. The power to change also lies within them. God has given man power to succeed in any chosen field. The force of nature will only act on which ever power you released.

"Now unto him who is able to do exceeding abundantly above all that we ask or think, according to the power that work in us" Eph3:20 KJV

To increase your value in life and become fruitful, depends on the power of choice within you. I will to end this book with the two stories, one an old story of two friends and secondly of one man who shock the in his time and his foot prints are everywhere for you to know that your destiny is in your hand. You're the product of the choice you make in life. Stop blaming others for all your errors and mistakes. That is the reason you've not make significant progress in that business, office or ministry. Learn to accept your faults and take responsibility for all your actions.

THE COBBLER TURNED FARMER

Two young men once visited a palm reader (astrologer). He told the first man "I can see a great man because he was born great, this man has a special oil of favor, that is why he has been experiencing favor from different people, he will rule his people' This was true of this man because people favor him more than his friends and siblings. The second man was quick to give out his hand to the man. After hearing what he told his friend. The man paused for a while and said hmmm...... *"I see a poor man; begging for food from neighbors, friends, families and serving his friend"*
Both of them left the place, the first man went home high shoulder up and started living big and enjoying favor from people as usual and being called a great man. While the second man couldn't say a word as they walked back home. The poor man thought throughout the night wondering why did God created him poor. They believed the words of the astrologer as God's word for their life. Because what he said was true to some extent.

The poor friend was a cobbler and his friend a food seller. He thought within himself "I've seen many food sellers becoming great but am yet to see shoe cobblers becoming great in this community". The idea of him serving his friend makes him sick daily. So he said to himself "I will rather become a farmer in the jungle than to serve my friend". He chose to relocated from that community and change his business.

Few weeks later, he sold off all he had to buy some grains and left the town with his family into the jungle, he built a hut and started farming. During the harvest season, he takes his crops to nearby villages and towns to sell and he devise a means to store those he couldn't sell. Soon his barn became big and people come to the jungle to buy from him rather than. So he stopped taking the foods out those villages.

There was a serious famine in the land and food become scarce, and the news went everywhere that there is a location somewhere in the jungle where there is enough food. The rich friend of this farmer came with other people from his home town and neighboring villages to buy grains and other foods from this cobbler turned farmer. He was surprised when he saw that the great farmer was his friend.

The farmer became the richest in that whole region and was given various chieftaincy titles by the neighboring towns and villages as well as free lands to farm. Many people wish their children and husbands to be like him. His fame went everywhere and became the envy of the society. The value of the cobbler turned farmer changed and his net worth increased. His friend later came to seek employment in one of his barn. All the words of the astrologer fell to the ground in this man's life. His choice and hard work changed things in his life. Diligence at work pay and increases your value and net worth.

This story reminds me a song sang be a musician sometimes ago. He said; anyone who dreamt of money and started celebrating his richest, he needs to be informed that he should be more diligent his work. If not, hunger is on the way." Surely the power to increase your value or net worth is in your hand, if you don't use it, it will be a waste and you will end up as no person in the society. Then you're a disappointment to God, humanity, those your friends you beat at the race of life in your mother's womb.

There are so many men around the world who has help transformed the secular world around and make it a more beautiful place than the one created by God in Genesis. Men who daily increase their value and increased their net worth in an astronomical way. The world is not complete without them because of the kind of choice they make. Men like Andrew Carnegie, Thomas Edison, Rockefeller, Henry Ford, Henry Heinz, Uncle Bens, Nikola Telsa Wright Brothers, John Walton, Elon Musk, Steve Job, Bill Gate, Mark Zuckerberg, etc.

JOHN DAVIDSON ROCKEFELLER

I choose him because of the uniqueness of his age and the way his vison has touched lives, his role in the church, philanthropy and his establishment is still doing well till today touching lives all over the world.

Born in Richford, New York, on July 8, 1839, John Davison Rockefeller moved with his family to Cleveland, Ohio, at the age of 14. Unafraid of hard work, he embarked on a number of small-business ventures as a teenager, landing his first real office job at age 16, as an assistant bookkeeper with Hewitt & Tuttle, commission merchants and produce shippers. By the age of 20, Rockefeller, who'd thrived at his job, ventured out on his own with a business partner, working as a commission merchant in hay, meats, grains and other goods. At the close of the company's first year in business, it had grossed $450,000.

A careful and studious businessman who refrained from taking unnecessary risks, Rockefeller sensed an opportunity in the oil business in the early 1860s. With oil production ramping up in western Pennsylvania, Rockefeller decided that establishing an oil refinery near Cleveland, a short distance from Pittsburgh, would be a good business move. In 1863, he opened his first refinery, and within two years it was the largest in the area. It didn't take much further success to convince Rockefeller to turn his attention full-time to the oil business.

STANDARD OIL COMPANY

In 1870, Rockefeller and his associates incorporated the Standard Oil Company, which immediately prospered, thanks to favorable economic/industry conditions and Rockefeller's drive to streamline the company's operations and keep margins high. With success came acquisitions, as Standard began buying out its competitors.

Standard's moves were so quick and sweeping that it controlled the majority of refineries in the Cleveland area within two years. Standard then used its size and ubiquity in the region to make favorable deals with railroads to ship its oil. At the same time, Standard got into the business itself with the purchase of pipelines and terminals, setting up a system of transport for its own products. Controlling (or owning) almost every aspect the business, Standard's grip on the industry tightened, and it even bought thousands of acres of forest for lumber and drilling and to block competitors from running their own pipelines.

Standard oil footprint got bigger as well, and it bought up competitors in other regions, soon pursuing ambitions of being an industry player both coast-to-coast in the U.S. and abroad. In just over a decade since Standard Oil was incorporated, it had a near monopoly of the oil business in the U.S. and consolidated each division under one giant corporate umbrella, with Rockefeller overseeing all of it. Everything Rockefeller had done to this point had led to the first American monopoly, or "trust," and it would serve as a guiding light for others in big business following behind him.

ANTITRUST ISSUES

With such an aggressive push into the oil industry, the public and the U.S. Congress took notice of Standard and its seemingly unstoppable march. Monopolistic behavior was not kindly regarded, and Standard soon became the epitome of a company grown too big and too dominant, for the public good. Congress jumped into the fray with both feet in 1890 with the Sherman Antitrust Act, and two years later the Ohio Supreme Court deemed Standard Oil a monopoly that stood in violation of Ohio law. Always eager to be a step ahead, Rockefeller dissolved the corporation and allowed each property under the Standard banner to be run by others. The overall hierarchy remained chiefly in place, though, and Standard's board maintained control of the web of spun-off companies.

Standard oil broke into 34 companies, top on these companies are Exxonmodil, Chevron, Amoco, ARCO, ConocoPhilp and others with many merges. Can you imagine the role of these companies in the economy of United States and other countries of the world where they are operating? Many homes and lives feeding from these countries all over the world today? This is a great life of value. His business empire stood out in the world today and the net worth of this man remain high. Generations to come will forever drink from the well of this man.

Just nine years after the company broke itself into pieces in the face of antitrust legislation, those pieces were again reassembled in a holding company. In 1911, however, the U.S. Supreme Court declared the new entity in violation of the Sherman Antitrust Act and illegal, and it was again forced to dissolve.

LATER YEARS AND LEGACY

Rockefeller was a devout Baptist, and once retired from the daily operations of running one of the world's largest businesses (in 1895, at age 56), he kept himself busy with charitable endeavors, becoming one of the more respected philanthropists in history. His money helped pay for the creation of the University of Chicago (1892), to which he gave more than $80 million before his death. He also helped found the Rockefeller Institute for Medical Research (later named Rockefeller University) in New York and the Rockefeller Foundation. In total he gave away more than $530 million to various causes.

Rockefeller passed away on May 23, 1937, in Ormond Beach, Florida. His legacy, however, lives on: Rockefeller is considered one of America's leading businessmen and is credited for helping to shape the U.S. into what it is today. His life insurance had to pay him huge amount of money because he lived many years without any breakdown on his health.

His only son, also named John, served by his father's side as a philanthropist while the elder Rockefeller was still alive and would continue his father's legacy of giving. During World War II he helped establish the United Service Organizations (USO), and after the war he donated land for the United Nations New York City headquarters. He also donated $5 million for the Lincoln Center for the Performing Arts in New York City, helped in the restoration of colonial Williamsburg, Virginia, and provided funding for the Museum of Modern Art. He gave 90% of his money to charity while alive making him one of the greatest philanthropist of all time. By this he was fulfilling the scripture that says *"One man gives freely, yet gains even more; another withholds unduly, but comes to poverty. A generous man will prosper; he who refreshes others will himself be refreshed."* Prov 11:24-25NIV

John. D. Rockefeller dedication, determination, diligence and commitment to his vision is very great which could be emulated by anyone in any field of live God has placed you. I brought these two stories for all of my reader to see that your background plays little or nothing about your life. The two men changed their story because they put to work all the ingredient that increase value and within a few years, everyone around them are bowing to them like Joseph.

Both men were not dubious, but a trustworthy and dedicated follower of God. One time I strongly believe is that God transfer wealth into their hand and the gave them the earth to dominate because they align their will with him. They never sit on their wealth as we have today among some rich people. Rockefeller use what he had to help others and the government of his time. That is why he for many years be a relevant man in the society. Instead of his corporation dying, they are growing stronger and stronger every year.

Beloved, if you do nothing you get nothing. The power to increase your value is within you. If you don't use it like the men I mention in this chapter, no one will use it for you. They all came from grass to grace. Most of them were not born with silver spoon. One major thing I wish to say is that everyone born into this world has all it takes to become great. If you don't, you have yourself to blame. Greatness, fame is in your blood. Both men whose story were shared above trusted God and believe in the abilities, power and potentials within them. Some didn't have education as most of us and doesn't have access to technology as we have today. But set their mind to change the world for good and God back them up. You can become whatever you choose to become like these men. Keep taking those positive steps that will increase your value daily, hope totally on God and soon you will become a great man in your society. See you on top of the ladder of success as one of the person that affected the world positivity.

Ref: https//www.biography.com, www. Wikipedia.com

RESOURCES FROM THE AUTHOR

A)   DAILY DEVOTIONAL

-    **THE SOUL BREAD DAILY DEVOTIONAL**: A monthly daily devotional to help members and Christians grow in faith and develop a habit of reading the Bible daily and regular communion with God and the Holy Spirit.

B)   MAGAZINE

-    **CHRISTIAN HERALDS:** A monthly news magazine for edification and spiritual developments of all Christians. It takes choice topics that affects people spiritual lives and daily well beings.

C)   OTHER BOOKS WRITTEN BY THE AUTHOR;

- Messed Up but Restored.

- The Fatherhood of God.

- Setting the Captives Free.

- Understanding Spiritual Authority.

- Praying Effective Prayer.

- Efficacy of Prayer.

- The Altar that Speaks.

- Increase Your Value (Net Worth).

- Stop Spending Time Invest Time.

- The Principle of Understanding.

- Securing Vision.

- What Do You Perceive?

- The Power of Choice.

- Grasshopper Mentality.

- The Truth and Realities of Life Vol 1.

- The Truth and Realities of Life Vol 2.

- Collections of Poems and Quotes.

- Harmony Essential Principle for Living.

- God's Battle Axe.

- The Mighty Hand of God.

D) EVANGELICAL TRACTS

If you have been blessed with this book and
needed personal, home / corporate (staff)
coaching supporting assistance,
spiritual clarity on some topics,
you can reach us at;

The Seekers of God International Church INC,
Rukpokwu, Port Harcourt, Rivers State.
Nigeria. West Africa.
Phone: +234 818 223 7323.
seekersworldmission@aol.com
seekersworldmission@aol.com

* 9 7 9 8 7 2 4 4 8 3 7 6 6 *